The Anthroposophical Society

The Anthroposophical Society

The Understanding and Continued Activity of the Christmas Conference

Edited by

Peter Selg & Marc Desaules

SteinerBooks | 2018

SteinerBooks
An imprint of Anthroposophic Press, Inc.
610 Main St., Great Barrington, MA 01230
www.steinerbooks.org

 Originally published in German as *Die Anthroposophische Gesellschaft. Beiträge zum Verständnis und zum Weiterwirken der Weihnachtstagung, Band 3* (Verlag des Ita Wegman Instituts, 2016).

Translated by Margot Saar

Book design by Jens Jensen

Financed by Lorene Allen

Library of Congress Control Number: 2017959581

ISBN: 978-1-62148-211-6 (paperback)

ISBN: 978-1-62148-212-3 (ebook)

Printed in the United States of America

Contents

Preface
by Marc Desaules and Peter Selg vii

1. The Existential Relationship with the Anthroposophical Society: Marie Steiner · Ita Wegman · Guenther Wachsmuth · Elisabeth Vreede · Albert Steffen
by Peter Selg 1

2. The Anthroposophical Society in Relation to the Spiritual World
by Stefano Gasperi 75

3. My Existential Relationship with the Anthroposophical Society
by Mario Betti 97

4. The Universal Temple
by J. Greiner 107

5. "Cosmic Midnight Hour": The Significance of the Mystery Dramas for the Anthroposophical Society
by Gioia Falk 123

6. The Evolving Body of the Anthroposophical Society
by Marc Desaules 139

Notes 163

Preface

Two and a half years ago, the Anthroposophical Society in Switzerland launched a series of conferences aimed at deepening the impulse of the 1923 Christmas Conference, the event that Rudolf Steiner himself referred to as a "festival of consecration" for the "beginning of a turning point of time."[1] The series celebrates the forthcoming centenary of this impulse by trying to develop a deeper understanding of the Anthroposophical Society's essential task and by actively and effectively contributing to shaping its future.

The research results and lectures as well as the artistic presentations of eurythmy and speech during this series of conferences at the Goetheanum are published in an extended and revised form to enable the readers, as individuals or in groups, to continue working with them. Following from the annual conferences of the Anthroposophical Society in Switzerland in 2014 and 2015 (entitled "The Social Structure of the Christmas Conference" and "The Foundation Stone and the Foundation Stone Meditation," respectively), the 2016 conference, held in Dornach from February 12 to 14, was entitled "The General Anthroposophical Society."

The idea behind this most recent conference was to let the Anthroposophical Society as an archetypal phenomenon speak to us. We hoped that the lectures and artistic contributions would make the existential relationship members have with the Anthroposophical Society tangible and that those gathered there would attain the capacity to consolidate the essence and future of this Society into free imaginations. It was not our intention to enter into new discussions on issues such as the Society's constitution or bylaws, however pertinent the problems and challenges associated with these issues continue to be.

We wrote in the introduction to the conference program:

> There is insufficient awareness, even in the heart of the anthroposophical community, of how significant a general anthroposophical society is for the future evolution of humankind. Rudolf Steiner created the forms of this model society from the flames of the first Goetheanum, as well as the imprints made by that event in the world ether. Built on a foundation stone that was sunk into the hearts of the members, where it has remained ever since, this innovative society then received its civilizing foundations in the bylaws that were discussed and amended with the members present and the representatives of the newly founded national societies. In taking that step the Anthroposophical Society planted, in the legal sphere and in the contemporary context, a seed of humanity and the model of a legal entity whose future potential and perspectives are yet to be discovered. It is a social organism that exhorts us to put our karma in order, carry what is close to our hearts into the world, and by doing so experience the presence and support of the divine spirit.
>
> Our relationship with the Anthroposophical Society can therefore not be neutral; people love it, hate it, or ignore it, but the relationship is always existential. At this annual conference we will try to come closer to

this reality, experience it through others, and discover it within ourselves.

This aim was clearly achieved in the main auditorium of the Goetheanum from February 12 to 14, 2016. From one lecture and artistic presentation to the next, the atmosphere condensed into a living and supporting being, and the members left the Goetheanum with full hearts and a stronger sense of initiative.

This book contains edited versions of lectures by Peter Selg, Stefano Gasperi, Mario Betti, Johannes Greiner, Gioia Falk, and Marc Desaules. We also asked various people (Mario Betti, Milena Kovarik, Rolf Brandt, Justus Wittich, and Danielle Lehmann) to give a brief personal account of their existential relationship with the Anthroposophical Society—in the Goetheanum's main auditorium, in front of the whole audience. This they all did in a very moving way. In the present volume we publish—*pars pro toto*—the contribution and subsequent question-and-answer session with Mario Betti. We thank him as well as all the organizers and members of this conference most warmly.

Marc Desaules and Peter Selg
October 2016

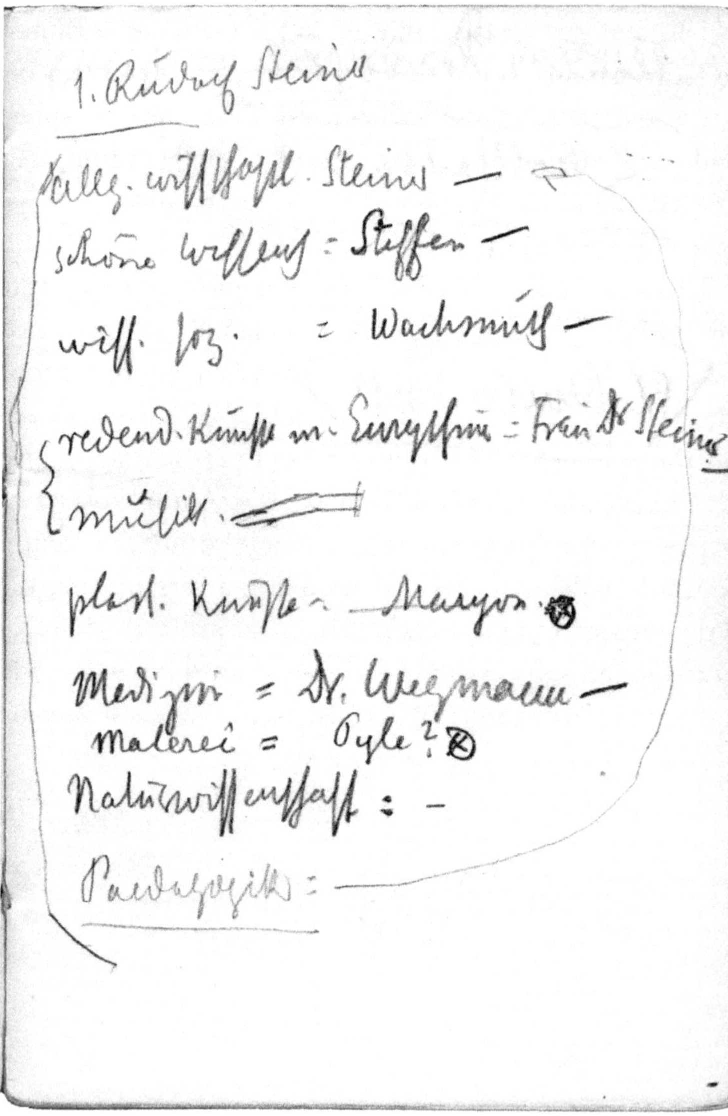

1. Rudolf Steiner

allg. wissenschaftl. Steiner —
schöne Wissensch. = Steffen —
wiss. soz. = Wachsmuth —
redend. Künste u. Eurythmie = Frau Dr Steiner
musik.
plast. Künste — Maryon
Medizin = Dr. Wegmann —
malerei = Pyle?
Naturwissenschaft : —
Paedagogik : —

Rudolf Steiner: Notebook entry, December 1923

1. The Existential Relationship with the Anthroposophical Society

Marie Steiner · Ita Wegman · Guenther Wachsmuth
Elisabeth Vreede · Albert Steffen

Peter Selg

In the years following the new foundation of the Anthroposophical Society in Switzerland in 1991, special editions of the Society's newsletter (*Mitteilungen aus dem anthroposophischen Leben in der Schweiz*) came out that focused on the "Original Executive Council," appointed in 1923, of the General Anthroposophical Society: the 1991 edition dealt with the Executive Council as a whole, while the 1993, 1995, 1997, 2000, and 2003 issues were dedicated to Albert Steffen, Marie Steiner-von Sivers, Ita Wegman, Guenther Wachsmuth, and Elisabeth Vreede, respectively. Ottfried Dörfler, who was general secretary of the Anthroposophical Society in Switzerland at the time, always composed the preface, his style marked by great clarity and warmth. It was important, he emphasized, to reflect on the tasks and the spiritual essence of the Anthroposophical Society in Switzerland, and to strive to better understand the impulse of the Christmas Conference to make this impulse "more potent." To achieve this, the members needed to be *jointly aware* of the spiritual situation and the tasks it posed, an awareness that would also form the foundation for the (continued) existence of the Goetheanum in Switzerland.

The original council of the General Anthroposophical Society and the council of the Society in Switzerland, he wrote, were initially identical. The Swiss Society was, after all, particularly close to the original council and to the General Anthroposophical Society. This small country, he said, had cosmopolitan ambitions, and its representative, the writer Albert Steffen, belonged to an Executive Council, whose members were born or had grown up in Austria (R. Steiner), Poland/Russia (M. Steiner-von Sivers), Indonesia (I. Wegman), Holland (E. Vreede), and Germany (G. Wachsmuth).

Remembering the dead could help us in the future, Ottfried Dörfler added that we would need their "strong forces from spirit lands" (R. Steiner). "*These people are most intimately connected with us.... With their spirit eyes they gaze upon us human beings of the present time, who are called upon to carry on, into the new century, with tasks they left unfinished. They are waiting for us to connect with them deeply and realize their renewed impulses on Earth.*"[1] Connecting ourselves in this way with the impulse of the Christmas Conference was, he continued, "true Michaelic service."[2]

Rudolf Steiner said that the members of the original Council of the General Anthroposophical Society would "work most closely with me here at the center [in Dornach]."[3] He made it clear from the start that this "closely working council" as a whole had an esoteric task, a fact we find expressed in his mystery drama *The Guardian of the Threshold*:

My pupils have unlocked their souls, each
in his own way, in order to receive
the spirit light according to his destiny.
What they have conquered for themselves
each one shall render fruitful for the others.[4]

The individual members need to unite, to form a higher unity that "*alone can waken to true life what otherwise / could merely stay as single bare existences.*"

So may their separate souls now join themselves
To sound in unison, attesting to the principle
Recorded in the book of cosmic destiny:
That harmony of spirits may achieve
what each alone could never bring about.[5]

When he founded the Anthroposophical Society in Cologne, Rudolf Steiner explained that this society should unite all human riddles within it.[6] Among these riddles was the failing of the original Council after 1925, the breakdown of "unity" and "harmony," the forsaking of the "principle recorded in the book of cosmic destiny," and the struggle and decline of the "brilliant five-pointed star" (Dörfler).

"*You will be scattered, each to his own, and leave me alone*" (John 16:32). In his poem *Patmos,* Friedrich Hölderlin wrote of the events unfolding after Christ's Ascension among the apostles and early Christians, "But it is fearful how God randomly / Scatters the living, here and there."[7] In a later version of the same hymn he even read the "scattering" as actual destruction that occurred *although* the disciples bore "great decisions" in their souls.

But it is truly fearful, how God randomly
smashes the living, here and there.[8]

This archetypal event repeated itself almost two millennia later in Dornach "at the beginning of the turning point of time." Albert Steffen once spoke of the "delineated competence" or rather "incompetence" of those involved. Into this, Anthroposophy was meant to enter like a "winged being," bringing liberation and opening. This it did, and yet, "The competence and incompetence... of each of us has also shaped the destiny of Anthroposophy, often acting as a hindrance or burden, dragging it down."[9]

Marie Steiner-von Sivers described the laying of the Foundation Stone for the Johannes Building in Dornach on September 20, 1913, as follows: "We were but a small gathering of poor people. Among us, one who was greater, one of those whom history only places at great intervals into turning points of time; one who subjected his will to the will of the spirit; who knew that he spoke to a time when evil held sway."[10] Certainly as a community—that is, in an important area that was pervaded by very destructive forces—the small gathering failed once the "great one" had passed away.

At Epiphany in 1948 (the year of her death), Marie Steiner-von Sivers highlighted this point, saying, "We are dealing with real adversarial forces that are stronger than even our best intentions."[11] After the disastrous General Meeting of 1935, she wrote, on April 14, to Elisabeth Vreede, who had been excluded from the Executive Council together with Ita Wegman, "All I can do now is say again how sorry I am that we were not able to come to an understanding. We have all suffered immensely because of this, and we will continue to suffer. With such sentiments, yet in remembrance of better days, I send my regards."[12]

The following deliberations will *not* address these "better days," nor will they dwell, yet again, on the crises and conflicts or on the various "karmic streams of humanity" to which the members of the original Executive Council belonged. Sergei O. Prokofieff, Erdmuth Grosse, and others have dealt with these questions, and the circumstances surrounding them are well known by now. Neither will they enlarge upon the "competence" or "incompetence" of individual persons, their achievements and failures, their propitious or ill-fated undertakings, their doing and suffering resulting from highest, mediocre, or lowest motives, nor on their previous existence as perpetrators or victims. But what will they be about?

We will be guided by the following question: What kept the devotion *to this society* alive in the members of the General Anthroposophical Society's original Executive Council? What, in the face of conflict and pain, did they consider to be their purpose? What did they see as their task in the face of a dramatically escalating world situation that did, in fact, absorb all the energy and strength people could muster? Where did they find the strength to carry on with their work in and for this Society—some, as in the case of Ita Wegman and Elisabeth Vreede, even after their exclusion? What was their wrestling for the being of the Anthroposophical Society like? What did this being mean to them? What was their perception of it? What was it about this being that was so important to them?

These are not only historical questions, problems, and worries; they are also highly relevant today and concern us directly. Why do *we* continue to invest so much time and energy in the Anthroposophical Society, a society that is losing members worldwide, that fails, in many countries, to attract young people, and is therefore largely unable to act? Why do we hold on to this "burden" instead of devoting our support, time, money, and commitment to other important initiatives and impulses? Why do we lavish our attention on what is often seen as a lost cause, a cause that is dying, as many people say who are convinced that the destructions of the past have long extinguished what Rudolf Steiner tried to achieve when he founded the Anthroposophical Society?

What keeps us here? Is it unwavering steadfastness and indestructible loyalty—or do we simply lack alternatives? Do we not find anything else to do, or is our loyalty born from a conscious decision? And is it really still true what Sergei O. Prokofieff once said and wrote: that the Anthroposophical Society is "the most important creation in the life and work of Rudolf Steiner"?[13] The most important creation ... more important than Anthroposophic Medicine and Waldorf education, the new approach to agriculture and nature study, the renewal of the sacramental acts of Christianity? Is *this* Society really more important than all these positive undertakings? Can we really and truly still say this? And if *yes*, why? We know that many people to whom Anthroposophy is important (if not everything) see this very differently. They would go with Rudolf Steiner's statement of February 27, 1923, his sixty-second birthday—if they knew it, which many don't considering all the historical oblivion. "The Anthroposophical Society," Rudolf Steiner said, "may appear differently in different eras, but Anthroposophy is independent of any anthroposophical society and can be found independently of such a society."[14] Not many know this citation, but they are familiar with the experience to which it refers, not from literature but from their own lives.

Precisely because of this situation the following reflections will examine the social ideals of the members of the original Executive Council. What did they stand and fight for in regard to the Society? What were their individual visions? Or: How was the being of the General Anthroposophical Society reflected in the "five-pointed star" of the *Vorstand*? We can assume, I think, that each of them not only wanted what was best, but that each of them did all they could to work toward this goal, to work toward their ideal of an anthroposophical society. "Believing in a person means feeling with that person's higher self," Albert Steffen once wrote.[15] This alone shall be our guiding principle. Why it all went wrong cannot be our question here—however crucial and vital a question that is. Sun ideals lived in each of them. And yet, their earthly personalities were often in their own and in each other's way—opening doors in their souls to destructive forces.

The following presentation does not give equal consideration to Marie Steiner-von Sivers, Elisabeth Vreede, Ita Wegman, Guenther Wachsmuth, and Albert Steffen, because their life's work—including their individual commitment to and struggle for the Anthroposophical Society (and their ideal of such a society)—has been investigated to varying degrees. Only in the case of Ita Wegman have all relevant sources been examined, and in recent years partly published. For Guenther Wachsmuth we have *almost no* personal documents because they have disappeared or been destroyed, a fact that makes it very difficult to say anything about the inner motives behind his lifelong devotion to the

Anthroposophical Society. With the other three personalities, the situation regarding their legacy lies somewhere between these two poles. Thus the history of the Society crisis from the point of view of the individual main agents has still not been reconstructed.

Nevertheless, the attempt shall be made to summarize what is known. The question as to whether or not such an attempt will be fruitful for the present or future of the Anthroposophical Society will have to remain open. Will this Society that Rudolf Steiner tried to establish with the Christmas Conference see new life and growth? "*Personally I think that one also has to give the miracle a chance to manifest*," Marie Steiner-von Sivers wrote on March 1, 1948.[16] She signed the very last letter she dictated almost ten months later, in the late hours of December 22, 1948, at Beatenberg, a village high above Lake Thun. This was her last day on Earth, a Wednesday, the day of Mercury, of merchants, but also of physicians. Again, her letter concerned—also—the Anthroposophical Society and the "evil spirit" that had pervaded it. And yet she wrote, "*I place my hope in the coming generation.*"[17]

I will begin the presentation proper of "the existential relationship with the Anthroposophical Society" with Marie Steiner-von Sivers, for two good reasons. She wrote in a letter on March 12, 1945, "I not only cofounded this Society; I also built it up branch after branch in accordance with Rudolf Steiner's anthroposophical movement until it was ready to become the Anthroposophical Society. I also did the work that led to the annexation of groups in other countries. This is why the Society has grown dearer to my heart than to anyone else's."[18] Rudolf Steiner confirmed this: "*I had to write things down, give lectures; Frau Doctor managed the entire Anthroposophical Society.*"[19] He pointed out that he could rely on Marie von Sivers in every respect when it came to building up the Society after the autumn of 1902, when it still belonged to the German Section of the International Theosophical Society: "[She] was the personality who, through her whole being, made it possible to keep our cause free from any trace of sectarianism. We owe it to her that our cause could become part of the general spiritual and cultural life."[20]

In fact, Rudolf Steiner and Marie von Sivers *together* built up the German Section of the Theosophical Society—the first manifestation of the Anthroposophical Society. Rudolf Steiner lectured, wrote books, traveled to work groups, spoke at annual meetings, and lent a sympathetic ear to everyone's concerns. Marie von Sivers conducted the correspondence with the branches and organized his trips and many other things. They even took on the publication and distribution of the Section's first journal, *Luzifer* (later *Lucifer–Gnosis*), together—down to writing addresses on envelopes and taking them to the mail office. The "annexation of groups in other countries" mentioned by Marie Steiner-von Sivers in her letter of March 1945 began early. The first journey abroad, at Easter 1904, took Rudolf Steiner and Marie von Sivers to Switzerland: three Swiss members had cofounded the German Section in Berlin two years earlier. He returned to this country as early as November 1905, when he gave public lectures and attended, with Marie von Sivers, the opening of a branch. During the same year, he visited Holland and England, where he held lectures, "drawing crowds," and inspiring them to work together on spiritual-scientific matters. Marie von Sivers often accompanied him on his foreign trips as his interpreter and close companion. But she also replaced him at "their" Berlin branch (founded by them together) while he was away, presented talks and introductions of her own, or read texts by him.

Rudolf Steiner expressly mentioned that Marie von Sivers was able to place the concerns of Anthroposophy and its society into the "general spiritual and cultural life." We must not forget how pitiful the situation was when Rudolf Steiner started in the fall of 1902. The theosophical movement in Germany had less than a hundred members when he became general secretary and began to organize them in a "Section." Most of these members had fallen out with one another; and there were some exotic if not strange characters among them. It was, as Marie von Sivers wrote in a letter at the time, like building a house "with mostly very poor materials"[21]—and the path toward a better future was long. *"It would be foolish to think that anything other than a broad spiritual movement could be of service,"* Rudolf Steiner said on August 14, 1906, four years after they had started to work together.[22]

The number of members and branches or study groups grew from year to year—slowly, but steadily. There was much that was petty and narrow-minded about the branches, much that only Rudolf Steiner's sense of humor, tolerance, and farsightedness were able to overcome. Even the successful performances of the mystery dramas in Munich, between 1910 and 1913, were quibbled over by the members because of the high production costs. At the second annual general meeting of the Anthroposophical Society in January 1914, Marie von Sivers defended these expenses, pointing out in her contribution that the performance of the dramas was of benefit for humanity and not only for the Anthroposophical Society. "Many of us are convinced," she added, "that these dramas will live longer than any building made of wood and stone."[23] History would prove her right.

The cradle of the Anthroposophical Society, the base and "headquarters" of the entire movement, was situated for a long time in a house in the second row on Motzstrasse 17, Berlin—an unpretentious and functional place of modesty, initiative, and enthusiasm, a place also of cultural earnestness. On November 9, 1923, in Dornach, Rudolf Steiner said good-bye to Anna Samweber, who had played an important part in the house in Motzstrasse, handing her a mantric verse—"To the Friends in Berlin"—to accompany them in the grim times that lay ahead. He drew three symbols on her forehead—a cross, the sign of Michael, and the Sun sign—and he said to her, "Sam, I need loyal, upright people. Stay upright and loyal." The following is an extract from the verse he gave her:

Humanity is forgetting
The innermost essence of God.
We will take it, though, and raise it
To the bright light of consciousness
And then bear over dust and ashes
The divine flame in the human heart.

Let lightning our sense houses
Shatter into dust:
We shall build soul-houses

Upon the iron-firm, weaving
Light of knowledge.
And outer downfall
Shall become the dawning
Of the innermost soul.[24]

For Marie Steiner-von Sivers *this* was the hallmark and mission of the Anthroposophical Society—people working together in this sense who felt connected with one another.

Édouard Schuré's withdrawal from the Society and his ugly vituperations in the summer of 1916, in the middle of the First World War, affected her deeply for the rest of her life. Aside from Rudolf Steiner he had been the person whom she had, esoterically, trusted and confided in most. She stepped down from the Central Council of the Society—"*Enough is enough...*"[25]

Later she spoke of the "ineffable burden" of the life and work after 1918, following a war that had destroyed so much and the failure of the Anthroposophical Society to keep up with its obligations. People were no longer united in the way they had been, the anthroposophical studies were beginning to lack spirit and focus, and life was becoming evermore hectic and chaotic. The steady times in Motzstrasse and the years of the mystery plays in Munich—Marie von Sivers' happiest time in and for the Anthroposophical Society—were gone; Dornach was and remained difficult, a thorny "hill of blood" in history.

Rudolf Steiner wrote to her on December 1, 1923,[26] that he "placed [his] *last* hopes on the gathering at Christmas." She was in Berlin, and he asked her to arrange for their joint apartment to be vacated and their publishing firm, the *Philosophisch-Anthroposophischer Verlag*, to be transferred to Switzerland. But it was not the end: things went on—or started anew. Rudolf Steiner asked her to join the newly formed Executive Council of the Anthroposophical Society as leader of the Performing Arts Section, a department of the School for Spiritual Science. He said during the conference that the history of the Anthroposophical Society itself had appointed her to this position.[27]

In the carpentry shop, at Easter 1924, Marie Steiner-von Sivers (as she was called after their marriage on December 24, 1914) recited the entire Foundation Stone Meditation for the first time. Rudolf Steiner had guided her personally and in greatest detail through aspects of word formation, syntax, emphasis, and intonation. Despite this spiritual initiative she went through immensely difficult times, marked increasingly by Rudolf Steiner's poor state of health and exhaustion. She saw the drama of his dying and of his death as a sacrifice taken on to save the Anthroposophical Society and movement: he took the painful fate of the society upon himself. The remaining Original Council then broke up twice, and Marie Steiner-von Sivers decided to withdraw to a former children's home at Beatenberg (Chalet Heimat). The purchase of this building had come into effect on September 1, 1939, the day when World War II started. She arranged for Rudolf Steiner's literary estate to be taken there as well as his urn, which remained there temporarily.

"*I must do my best to preserve Dr. Steiner's work in accordance with his intentions.*" This statement of September 15, 1948, three months before her demise, encapsulated what had been the guiding principle of Marie Steiner-von Sivers' life and work during her final years.[28] She saw

Anthroposophy and the Anthroposophical Society as an incomplete work for the future, "a work that needs to lead the fourth into the sixth cultural era and that could only be attempted presciently by a relatively small group of people in the fifth cultural era."[29] *Small group, attempted,* and *presciently*—her view of the Anthroposophical Society and community is reminiscent of Christian Morgenstern's description in his letter to Marie Goettling thirty-five years earlier on December 20, 1913, in which he wrote about the importance of creating "islands of spiritual life" for the future. ("Just look at today's world; compare it with your youth. Wait another fifty or eighty years, and the bleakness will be so ubiquitous that you would not have the will to live were it not for a few islands of spiritual life; if there weren't at least a small minority of people *preparing* for that time."[30])

Marie Steiner-von Sivers had long hoped that the Anthroposophical Society and movement, the School for Spiritual Science, and the anthroposophical arts would be more effective and achieve more than the creation of "islands of spiritual life." And yet, she did not give up hope altogether. She sensed the "immense potency of Dr. Steiner's work" and invested all the energy she still had in its preservation. By publishing an edition of Rudolf Steiner's entire writings and lectures that was as complete as possible, she wished to present the entirety and structure of his work for future generations to make "their own." She said of the Anthroposophical Society in retrospect that it had been unable to protect Rudolf Steiner and his work. This did not prevent her, however, from continuing to feel part of that failing society: "We have let Dr. Steiner down in so many respects and there is much for which we need to make amends."[31] She stated unequivocally that the individual anthroposophists and the Anthroposophical Society as a whole were to blame for his death. Rudolf Steiner's work was able to protect itself to a certain extent—but his much-attacked earthly personality would have needed the esoteric support of an awakened community that never materialized.

Marie Steiner-von Sivers spent her final days and died far from Dornach, but she never stopped caring about the Goetheanum building, the Anthroposophical Society, and its School for Spiritual Science. She found it difficult to come to terms with the low spiritual and artistic standards that had slipped in at the Goetheanum, spoke of conventional "practices of the theatre world" having been introduced, and thought that only the conscious return to Rudolf Steiner's guidelines could bring "healing."

In a letter of January 6, 1948, Marie Steiner-von Sivers described the Society's barren esoteric life, but also pointed out that "remarkable individual attempts" were being made. While these were mostly artistic endeavors, "the possibility of a regeneration of our esoteric life might well lie that way."[32] The anthroposophical arts, which had become quite advanced in the very first decade of the anthroposophical movement, might be able to bring about a change. The overall goal was not the internal work, but a positive Anthroposophy that would reach out into the world. ("Marie von Sivers was *the* personality who, through her whole being, made it possible to keep our cause free from any trace of sectarianism. We owe it to her that our cause could become part of the general spiritual and cultural life...")

Marie Steiner-von Sivers pointed out toward the end of her life, when she looked back from Beatenberg, that the Goetheanum was not been destroyed but fell victim to Ahriman. People urgently needed to become less self-interested if they wished to be truly able to serve Anthroposophy. Marie Steiner-von Sivers tried to build on the goals and motives that had guided Rudolf Steiner in 1912 when he founded the "Society for Theosophical Method and Art," although she knew full well how difficult these were to achieve. "If we continue to seek ways toward this goal, we must never leave the path of truth, we must practice tolerance, and support any valuable positive endeavor," she wrote on September 3, 1947.[33] Focusing on the truth was fundamental, she said; any internal peace settlement or tolerance not founded on the truth would not lead forward. After all the crises and tragedies, the need for harmony within the Anthroposophical Society was great; and yet, it would not be possible in her view to move beyond the disasters the Society had experienced if they had not been worked through and understood. The problems had not started only after Rudolf Steiner's death but long before. She invested her final efforts in publishing any material available on the subject. "It was no easy decision," she wrote, "to uncover the sins and weaknesses of the Society for the sake of the movement and Dr. Steiner's intentions."[34]

She certainly did not think that tolerance toward all the "positive work" in support of Anthroposophy implied universal and unconditional "openness." What was needed instead was an unambiguous assessment of what "positive endeavor" actually meant: without that kind of judgment and the courage to apply it, there could be no real progress within the Anthroposophical Society and the School for Spiritual Science. The fight had to go on against the influences that "keep trying to undermine the rigor and purity of Rudolf Steiner's method of spiritual-scientific research and to push the Society in the direction of psychic sensationalism."[35] Ever since 1902, Marie Steiner-von Sivers had suffered from this "psychic sensationalism" and from the leaning of some Society members in that direction. She had witnessed its most bizarre manifestations, including abstruse claims regarding former lives and all kinds of paranormal experiences and pretensions. All this was not helpful to the Society, and she thought it wrong to tolerate these phenomena, however "socially" attractive they might seem.

She did not give up, and during the summer of 1948 she wrote of the Goetheanum, "There is quite an outward bustle now in Dornach, whereas much is wrong within. There is nevertheless also a sense that the work needs to be preserved and that it might blossom again at the end of the century."[36] She remained convinced of this until the end of her life in spite of crises and alienations, and this view also extended to the Society. She did not think that the Anthroposophical Society and movement would see their "culmination" at the end of the twentieth century, and she knew all too well that Rudolf Steiner had made a potential "culmination" dependent on conditions of which none had materialized (including the understanding and application of the Christmas Conference, the karma lectures, etc.). She did believe that a "*blossoming*" of Anthroposophy at the end of the twentieth century—despite all the declining developments of the past—was possible, and she was open to new approaches. It was important, she emphasized, "to become more tolerant and broad-minded than we would like to be," because this was what the future demanded.

Nothing less than the "liberal impulses of Dr. Steiner"[37] were at stake, and it was therefore important "to open our hearts more and more to the free [anthroposophical] initiatives," she wrote on March 30, 1948, the twenty-third anniversary of Rudolf Steiner's death.[38] "It seems to me necessary at this point in time always to appreciate goodwill as a positive force and to be aware of what the times ask of us. Of course, the emerging standpoints will be different from the ones that prevailed before the war, because the world has become more radical and the new generation has been shaped by entirely different forces and circumstances. We, who constitute a last transitional layer, have to see how we can build a bridge from the past to the future so that there is spiritual continuity."[39]

With this in mind, Marie Steiner-von Sivers decided to agree to the publication of Rudolf Steiner's lectures on historical topics by a non-anthroposophic publisher (Europa), a decision that provoked storms of indignation within the Anthroposophical Society. But she was not perturbed by this response—"I think it is wrong to bury within a sect the words Dr. Steiner directed at today's people and humanity."[40]

All these were future-oriented and viable thoughts and visions, signs of light and warmth at the end of Marie Steiner-von Sivers' life—particularly with regard to the Anthroposophical Society. Remaining positive was a struggle, however, and she often looked to the Society and the Goetheanum with melancholy, if not despair—"Dr. Steiner's work, of which the Goetheanum has to be seen as the center." What she saw was "a caricature of what Anthroposophy should have achieved and *what we now need to begin to seek anew.*"[41] At Christmas 1942, two decades after a horrendous blaze destroyed the first Goetheanum, which was insufficiently protected by the Society, she wrote to the members for the last time: "What can be done when a society that has taken on the sacred historical task to protect and promote a work without which humanity can only degenerate is caught up in problems it cannot resolve?"[42] The existence of the Anthroposophical Society was at stake, she wrote, in the midst of war and misery and a severe internal crisis. Its moral substance needed to be rescued and strengthened; people had to summon the will to forgive and to attempt a new start: "The words *only what is fertile is true* can be our inspiration. We must be able to work together again, in harmony and without excluding those we dislike. We must not deny anyone who is loyal to the cause and to Rudolf Steiner the chance to work with us."

Referring to the end of Rudolf Steiner's life, she continued, "Looking at his sacrifice and death, for which we bear the blame, individually and as a society—because he took our karma upon himself—can we not forget and forgive and open our doors wide to those who seek?" This alone, she felt, could bring about a catharsis "for the Society and the individuals." "I say this in full awareness of the weight of these words, in full awareness of the fact that I will most likely soon have to step before Rudolf Steiner's spiritual form. Let us salvage his work and his cultural gift to humanity by overcoming our reservations and by reconciling, by opening our doors wide to those who seek."

After this appeal Marie Steiner-von Sivers had six years left to work in the way outlined by her: to promote Anthroposophy and Rudolf Steiner's work, but also the Anthroposophical Society, which, she thought, occupied such a central place in this work. What the future needed was "*a society that knew its tasks and was aware of its responsibilities as a community,*"[43] a society that would constantly strive toward this goal: "Nothing is more difficult than educating people toward communal awareness."[44] Fred Poeppig and Marie Savitch, who visited her in Beatenberg, wrote about her final days, "To her very last day she was preoccupied with the destiny of the Anthroposophical Society" (Poeppig).[45] "The conflicts that had shaken the Society in recent years were very remote to her now. She 'had nothing more to do' with them. Instead, she remained as deeply connected as ever to the true spirit of the Society, which is associated with Rudolf Steiner" (Savitch).[46] The very first verse Steiner had ever given her for a festive recitation includes these lines:

Behold the Sun
At the midnight hour,
And build with stones
In lifeless ground.

So find in downfall
And in death's dark night
Creation's new beginning,
and morning's youthful might.[47]

Much less is known of Elisabeth Vreede's relationship with the Anthroposophical Society and her ideal of what that society should be than in Marie Steiner-von Sivers' case. "*It won't be long before I will be forgotten*," she said wisely[48]—and this turned out to be true. In the end, her house and her garden (and indirectly her ashes, which are buried there) were sold by the anthroposophists. In 2009, the Year of Astronomy and the sixty-sixth anniversary of her death, her name was barely mentioned, even in Dornach. She was shy, as Madeleine van Deventer, who knew her well, pointed out, and she rarely spoke about herself or her inner life. On the other hand, Emanuel Zeylmans van Emmichoven, Ita Wegman's biographer, stated that, because of her absolute "authenticity," he'd had the most profound experience of the consciousness soul with her.[49]

Elisabeth Vreede's steadfastness was an example to many people in the Anthroposophical Society, even if they did not—or did not dare to—admit this, because Dr. Vreede had by that time been excluded and become a *persona non grata*. She was a "rock" one could build on, said the writer Dora Krück von Poturzyn,[50] who knew much about the Knights Templar, and she continued to be that "rock" even after everything was taken away from her at the Annual General Meetings in 1934 and 1935: the leadership of the Section for Mathematics and Astronomy (including responsibility for the observatory and Section newsletters), her membership in the Executive Council, and the Rudolf Steiner Archives, which she herself had set up at the Goetheanum. All the members of the Executive Council suffered grievously from the conflicts and divisions—but none of them lost their entire professional and anthroposophical existence in the way Elisabeth Vreede did. Yet she never lost sight of her path. "*I will decide for myself what my attitude will be*," she said at the Annual General Meeting in 1934 to an overwhelming majority of people who had voted against her.[51]

Madeleine van Deventer spoke of an "ancient element of wisdom" that permeated Vreede's much-tried being and her assessment was certainly very close to the truth.[52] Dr. Vreede was a "very old member," Rudolf Steiner said jokingly at the Christmas Conference,[53] but he was not referring to her age (she was only forty-four at the time) and not only to the fact that she had been involved very early on with the German Section of the Theosophical Society. "A very old member." For Elisabeth Vreede it was this sense of humor that was "so liberating about the spiritual life"—another aspect that had brought her particularly close to Rudolf Steiner.

Elisabeth Vreede did join the Theosophical Society at a young age (she was only twenty-one) after growing up in a theosophically oriented family. Colonel Olcott who, in 1875, had founded the Theosophical Society with Helena Petrovna Blavatsky in New York, was a frequent guest in her parental home in The Hague, and Rudolf Steiner gave anthroposophical lectures and esoteric lessons there. After the foundation of the Anthroposophical Society, Elisabeth Vreede's mother was the first branch leader in The Hague (from 1913).

Elisabeth joined the Theosophical Society in 1900 although she felt, as she wrote later, an inner resistance: "Something in me rebelled the more against it as I had the feeling that not even the most violent resistance would be of any use; there is a force that is stronger than you are in your ordinary consciousness, and this force is directing you there. I had known such forces in my life, but was not used to them placing me into something so impenetrable."[54] Her anthroposophical breakthrough came when she heard Rudolf

Steiner's lectures on *The Theosophy of the Rosicrucian* in Munich in 1907: "In these lectures I experienced nothing of the dissatisfaction that the theosophical teachings always left me with. What Rudolf Steiner presented there was scientifically comprehensible and convincing. The longing for the spirit found its fulfillment in spiritual insight."[55]

Elisabeth Vreede was a self-declared hermit and a very intelligent woman, mathematician, and astronomer with an amazing memory and broad knowledge of philosophy. She was, however, not a real hermit, but quite sociable—*"gezellig,"* as the Dutch would say. She longed for Rudolf Steiner's Spiritual Science and affirmed it with the powers of her own spiritual intelligence. And she was deeply impressed by what she experienced as a spiritual community or "communal spirit" (Hegel) when she listened to the lectures and esoteric lessons of the Anthroposophical Society as it was evolving—*through this spirit.*

After 1907, she was present at all the essential lectures and stages of the Anthroposophical Society, as long as they were connected with Rudolf Steiner. Without a family, financially independent, and in full command of her mental faculties she devoted herself wholly to the emerging Anthroposophical Society under Rudolf Steiner. She, too, lived temporarily in Motzstrasse 17 before moving to Dornach in 1914, at the age of thirty-five, to help with the building work there. She was a founding member, secretary of the branch at the Goetheanum, and part of the Council of the Anthroposophical Society in Switzerland, which had been founded in the fall of 1920—at the time of the Goetheanum opening—as an independent national society.

Vreede helped organize conferences at the Goetheanum and managed the registrations and accounts. She also established (under her own steam and with her own money) the Rudolf Steiner Archives at the Goetheanum, where members and interested visitors could see or even borrow Rudolf Steiner's writings and lecture transcripts. She created a place of deepening, where people could study, and ask questions about, Rudolf Steiner's work. Having an amazing overview of Steiner's complete work, Elisabeth Vreede was always willing to help. Her Rudolf Steiner Archives were a site of the Anthroposophical Society in the best sense of the word: *no dust* gathered there because they were in constant use. "This seemed to me to be the hallmark of anthroposophical archives," she wrote later[56]– after these archives, too, had been taken away from her and dissolved.

Elisabeth Vreede was the first anthroposophist who, in 1919, gave lectures in England on social threefoldness. She was also a close friend of Edith Maryon. She promoted the distribution of Rudolf Steiner's *Appeal to the German People and the Cultural World* in the Netherlands and in Switzerland. Years later, after the Goetheanum fire, she started (on January 1, 1923, one day after the fire) a reconstruction fund, organized fundraising, and, together with her family, donated a considerable sum herself. The inner, esoteric work and support were, however, equally important to her. She was among the few who understood that the Goetheanum had become vulnerable as a result of the community's lack of spirituality and the failing of the Anthroposophical Society. She wholeheartedly welcomed the new beginning at the Christmas Conference and Rudolf Steiner's appearance there. She fully agreed with his words: that it was even more important from then on to act "fully guided by the truth," because the spiritual world expected this of humanity "in the various areas of life."[57] To "follow the impulses from the spiritual world in clarity and truth"[58] was precisely what she intended to do. She felt greatly honored when Rudolf Steiner appointed her to the original Executive Council of the General Anthroposophical Society, despite the fact that she was not a prominent anthroposophist and lecturer. She was overjoyed when he established a Section for Mathematics and Astronomy at the new School, and when he handed that Section over to her. That the spiritual-scientific exploration of astronomy was one of his major concerns she had known for a long time. "Understanding human life out of the universe through living knowledge—that is...what Spiritual Science strives for today."[59]

The depth of Elisabeth Vreede's internalization and understanding of the Christmas Conference and its intentions is reflected in the lecture she gave on October 2, 1928, at the opening of the second Goetheanum. Speaking on "The Impulse of Christmas and Michael," she said that the Anthroposophical Society had been founded at the Christmas Conference in accordance with the laws of the spiritual world. Its Christmas character lay in the fact that it had come to the Earth from the spiritual world.

One of the main qualities of the Christmas Conference was the color-creating encounter and interpenetration of outer and inner, of light and darkness, qualities that were also reflected in its bylaws and spiritual principles. She also emphasized the importance of Rudolf Steiner's signature on the members' cards: spiritual *and* earthly requirements needed to be considered if the spiritual impulse was to become active in the *physical* world. Section 9 of the bylaws described the relationship between the Anthroposophical Society (as an organ in the physical world) and the School for Spiritual Science (as a spiritual being) "in a wonderfully clear way." The relationship between the General Anthroposophical Society and the national societies had also been illuminated. Now, after Rudolf Steiner's death, it was important to continue to respect the spiritual laws in Dornach and in the anthroposophical work worldwide and to keep the connection with the spiritual world alive. Rudolf Steiner had perceived these "spiritual laws" clearly, Vreede said, but since his passing into the spiritual world they could only be "sensed."

Maintaining and continuing the Christmas Conference therefore needed great courage and the occult-esoteric capacity to adapt to the spiritual world. Most important of all was the connection with the world of the dead. Rudolf Steiner's deeds, the Christmas Conference included, opened a "gateway" into the spiritual world. All this required active involvement, but also an honest and open admittance of former mistakes. Anthroposophists needed to apply the Michael impulse in practice and adhere to the intentions Rudolf Steiner had expressed when he said, "Here [in Dornach], we want to gain the strength to pursue the impulses from the spiritual world."[60] "Those who wish to represent the anthroposophical movement in a dignified way must come to know that the spiritual impulses also apply to the Anthroposophical Society itself."[61]

On October 2, 1928, Elisabeth Vreede asked in the main auditorium of the Goetheanum, "*Do we have a Society that is able to rightly express the inner, the esoteric, in this exoteric world, a society whose intentions are in line with those of the founder of this movement?*"[62] She did not answer these questions negatively; but it was clear where she saw the need for action and a more future-oriented thinking. We do not know how her lecture was received and what kind of response it elicited. I published her for the first time, directly from her literary estate (in The Hague) in my monograph on the occasion of the sixty-sixth anniversary of her death in 2009. To my knowledge it was unknown, or had been forgotten, in the other centers of the Anthroposophical Society.

Looking back, Elisabeth Vreede described even the situation of the Executive Council *with* Rudolf Steiner up until March 30, 1925, as difficult. The spiritual teacher was, she said, fully occupied with tidying up the "old debris" in the Anthroposophical Society[63]—and hardly any time was given over to the new impulses in their meetings. There were strong oppositional views right from the start. Marie Steiner-von Sivers never accepted Ita Wegman and had generally a problem with the fact that she no longer led the Anthroposophical Society alone with Rudolf Steiner but had become one of a group. Vreede spoke of a "painful and sad time" for the Executive Council between January 1924 and March 1925. She herself had always tried after Steiner's death to maintain the unity of this body and refrained from siding with any particular faction.

At the 1935 Annual General Meeting she said, "I declare that I have made every effort in more than ten years to do *my duty as a member of the Executive Council with the greatest responsibility*, under immensely difficult circumstances."[64]

Elisabeth Vreede, however, experienced a strong "will for destruction" within the Anthroposophical Society, directed at herself and at Ita Wegman. Wilhelm Kelber, a devoted Christian Community priest spoke of the "brutality of the persecution" directed at Vreede and complained in Dornach about the inflammatory propaganda and speeches of anthroposophists such as Roman Boos, Curt Englert, and Hans W. Zbinden; deeply shaken by these lectures, he went as far as speaking of "executions."[65]

Vreede herself remained reserved. When the Swiss anthroposophist Karl Ballmer advised her in March 1935 to take legal steps against her imminent exclusion from the Executive Council at the annual general meeting, she repudiated his advice and the tone of his well-intended letter. "*What is missing: love as a cognitive organ*," she wrote in the margins of his letter, and replied on March 30, 1935, the tenth anniversary of Rudolf Steiner's death: "One cannot call Mr. Steffen a Judas, or Mrs. Steiner a 'person,' while pretending to do something to improve the situation inside the Society." One-sidedness was wrong, she wrote, and it was important to remain open to other truths: "To find these truths, we must develop the true, universal human *love* into a cognitive organ as described by Rudolf Steiner."[66]

Instead of a general meeting, Elisabeth Vreede would have preferred an independent inquiry into the conflicts of the Executive Council and the accusations raised against her. She understood the dynamics at work that, in the sub- or supraconsciousness of the protagonists, aimed to destroy the work of Rudolf Steiner—all this at a time of historical decisions and with fascism ascending. Elisabeth Vreede wished, and was obliged, to defend herself, just like Ita Wegman and many others. And yet she wrote, "What we wish to achieve with these refutations and so on is to awaken insight in the others... so that they see the mistakes they have made. And I feel just as strongly that it is our spiritual duty not to desert our—now truly misguided—brothers, not to make the division complete."[67] Vreede spoke of (misguided) "brothers and sisters" and was not willing to give up on the Anthroposophical Society as an esoteric community, not even at the time of its greatest darkness and aberration. With her love for the impulse of the Christmas Conference she actively supported the continuation of anthroposophical activities and worked with the corresponding groups in other countries. She even headed the central communication bureau of the "United Free Anthroposophical Groups" after 1935.

As early as 1932 she had spoken of the need for all positive forces in the anthroposophical movement to unite, pleading strenuously for "magnanimity." If that was achieved the Anthroposophical Society could be a much bigger and much more powerful movement. Important parts of the anthroposophical movement had been excluded from the Society since Rudolf Steiner's death. "*Unity* alone cannot reach the highest goals, if this unity refuses to see the other side."[68]

In 1938, three years after she was herself excluded from the Executive Council and had to give up all aspects of her work at the Goetheanum, Elisabeth Vreede wrote in an essay, *On the Anthroposophical Work,* that the anthroposophical movement (which began in Berlin in 1902) had now passed its thirty-fifth year. From now on spiritual influences would be more effective than the physical. It was important for the anthroposophical impulse to unfold its activity in the world. Although she knew how precarious the situation was, she appeared optimistic about the medium- and long-term developments, saying that the anthroposophical movement "will become better and better at radiating out its spiritual forces into the world, and the effect of these forces will gain momentum and maturity so that pure spirit can permeate the entire movement."[69] Elisabeth Vreede did not speak of the Anthroposophical Society but of the anthroposophical movement—and yet she never gave up her hope for the future of the Society. If the movement could be permeated by "pure spirit," then the Society could regain importance. "*The being of Anthroposophy—I have always felt that it is a spiritual being newly created by Dr. Steiner: the first hierarchical being created by a human being, as it were, very young and still incomplete, like an infant—a being that now has to grow up, through our working together as a 'community of knowledge' and with help from its creator in the spiritual world.*"[70]

For Elisabeth Vreede the composition of the original Executive Council of the General Anthroposophical Society meant that Marie Steiner-von Sivers and she herself, as "old members," brought spiritual continuity; Guenther Wachsmuth and Albert Steffen, who had no connection with the Society's origin and tradition, constituted the opposite pole, while Rudolf Steiner and Ita Wegman represented the "*directly active spiritual principle*" in the esoteric Council at the time of the Christmas Conference.[71]

Ita Wegman was three years older than Elisabeth Vreede and nine years younger than Marie Steiner-von Sivers. She had come to Rudolf Steiner in Berlin in 1902 and, like Marie von Sivers and Elisabeth Vreede, she had belonged to the German Section of the Theosophical Society from the beginning. However, unlike her two future colleagues on the Executive Council, she soon left Berlin and never worked on the Goetheanum building site, because she had other tasks and duties, primarily the study of medicine at Zurich and the setting up of a medical practice there in 1917. She went to Switzerland first—ahead of the anthroposophical movement—but remained always in contact with Rudolf Steiner and the anthroposophical community around him. She was active in the Zurich branch, invited Rudolf Steiner there, and was a member of his esoteric school.

In 1907, at the International Whitsun Congress of the Theosophical Society in Munich, when the two esoteric schools split apart, she decided resolutely in favor of him and his path ("I will stay with you"), leaving behind her Dutch friends, most of whom supported Annie Besant and had no real understanding of the spiritual situation. "Then his eyes lit up, he took my hand, gave me the sign of Michael, and said important things to me."[72] The further path of Ita Wegman's life and work that, after the fire, led her into the closest companionship with Rudolf Steiner, also unfolded *in signum Michaeli*. She stood by his side at the abyss, awakened with his help to his and her karmic situation, and was an indispensable companion and supporter to him up until March 30, 1925.

> I shall be supported
> By your understanding
> Your love and faithfulness.
> I see arising from your understanding,
> the light that shines for me,
> I see arising from your love
> the warmth that blesses me

I see arising from your faithfulness
the air that enlivens me

This was one of many verses he wrote down for her.[73]

Ita Wegman experienced Rudolf Steiner's struggle for the possible regeneration of the Anthroposophical Society from close proximity, fully aware also of how intensely he had struggled for such a society before the fire. "*This is what I keep asking our friends, because we are faced today with the need to turn the Society into a being that is active and effective in the world*" (The Hague, Nov. 1922).[74]

Rudolf Steiner had pointed out repeatedly before and after the fire that the Anthroposophical Society had to carry the anthroposophical movement. Consolidating and modernizing the Society was of prime importance so that it could become a positively effective force in the world. How often had Rudolf Steiner mentioned in previous years that people needed to learn to see, and be alert to, the present and future misery in the world, and to the tasks arising for them in this situation—tasks "that people outside can also respect."[75] This possibility and the responsibility of the Anthroposophical Society, domestically as well as internationally, concerned Ita Wegman deeply. It had to be possible to work from Dornach across national borders and in all areas of life on behalf of the anthroposophical impulses of resurrection.

Rudolf Steiner said often, "There has to be a much stronger cohesion, a working together of anthroposophists in all countries. An understanding across the whole world is possible through and for the sake of Anthroposophy."[76] Ita Wegman knew that Rudolf Steiner was not only thinking of the need to disseminate the anthroposophical worldview and the anthroposophical image of the human being (as well as the spiritual-scientific path of development), but also of the specialist areas, such as medicine, in which she was primarily interested. It was Ita Wegman who, six months after the Dornach fire, asked Rudolf Steiner about the establishment of an esoteric school at the Goetheanum—and who spoke to him of her longing for a mystery medicine, a medicine informed by the new mysteries of an esoteric Christianity. These questions and her initiative were instrumental in inspiring the idea of the Christmas Conference, of the new foundation of the Anthroposophical Society and the School for Spiritual Science at the Goetheanum, with an esoteric school that would be implemented in the various "areas of life," including medicine. Like Elisabeth Vreede, Ita Wegman supported the reconstruction of the Goetheanum in every way she could.

On June 1, 1923, she wrote to Gracia Ricardo, who was working in the United States, "If Dr. Steiner had a million he could start and we would soon have a Goetheanum again, which is so very important for the future progress of our movement. The carpentry shop proved much too small for the recent teachers' course, because so many people came to it. We do not want to be a society that is so pathetic that it does not even have a proper building for receiving the people who are interested in Anthroposophy. We are honor-bound to do this for Dr. Steiner. I therefore ask you, too, to bring this matter to the attention of prominent personalities and let them know that we are determined to build again."[77]

Ita Wegman was willing to do everything in her power to help "the principles of the Christmas Conference to break through" in the Anthroposophical Society.[78] Together with Rudolf Steiner, and using the example of medicine and curative education, she demonstrated how a section of the School for Spiritual Science could be developed and led in practice, research, teaching, and training. She also took the First Class training course very seriously, for which she had shared responsibility. Rudolf Steiner would talk Ita Wegman through each class lesson on the evening before, explain its composition, and write the mantras down for her. She had to be optimally prepared—and she always was! For Ita Wegman the new foundation of the Anthroposophical Society was a pivotal and fundamental deed. She was present when Rudolf Steiner decided to start over with the vessel that was so important but that had neglected its duties so tragically over the recent years. Later, Ita Wegman spoke of the Anthroposophical Society as having been "forged again into a unity by the Christmas Conference."[79]

With the Christmas Conference, Rudolf Steiner established the basis for a "unified awareness" within the Anthroposophical Society (and the Michael movement active in it) of how to tend to the tasks entrusted to it—by laying the Foundation Stone in a mystery act; by founding the esoteric school as the "core" and "soul" of the Society and the "rock" of Anthroposophy; by presenting the karma lectures, the "Leading Thoughts," the letters to members, and essays in the *Newsletter;* and in many other ways.

The lessons of 1923 had to be learned but, in the years following Rudolf Steiner's death, Ita Wegman found she was alone in the Executive Council with the task of implementing this new start in the Society. "As you know it was impossible to put into practice what Rudolf Steiner had in mind when he called for a Christmas Conference. There was rather strong resistance from the very beginning, *and he knew this directly after the act had been performed at the Christmas Conference.* We then fought for ten years to bring the principles of the Christmas Conference to a breakthrough. Unfortunately the opposition was so strong that nothing could be achieved...," she wrote later.[80]

Ita Wegman did all that was in her power after 1925 to prevent such an outcome (which had looked likely from the beginning), and she was determined to lead the Anthroposophical Society, which Rudolf Steiner had newly founded with such devotion and energy, toward its ideal, against all odds and in the face of any opposition—although she could have done her work in medicine and special needs education much better *without* this Society with its time-consuming and draining meetings and conflicts. As early as 1930, five years before she was excluded from the Executive Council and five years after Rudolf Steiner's death, half-way through the ten-year tenure of the Original Council, she wrote in a letter,

> Everything hangs by a thread; it will depend on the wakefulness of a number of people whether this thread, which connects us with R. St. [Rudolf Steiner], will tear altogether. The tasks [of] R. St.'s individuality are certainly immense and comprise more than just leading a community of people. But if this community does not achieve its goals, it will, as a complex of forces, become a dreadful obstacle for anyone belonging to it, and will even have a destructive effect on world evolution. We are not taking this future image seriously. We think that we don't want to have too much to do with the [Anthroposophical] Society. We are much too prone to such thinking. I have realized that such thinking is neither right nor truthful. A number of us need to do what R. St. expected of the Society. We must connect with each other so that we can take on the

> spiritual work, so that we can carry the new impulse into the world—not just theoretically, but in practice! The light that will then be able to shine will be health giving and helpful for the people in the Society and for those who are gradually finding their way to it. This is what Michael admonishes me to do: to illumine dark places. And I find these dark places mostly in the Society, where they are the darker and harder to bear because there used to be light.[81]

However, the possibility of Ita Wegman doing something for the Anthroposophical Society as a whole was limited. Shortly after Rudolf Steiner's death she had already tried to continue with the motifs of the "Leading Thoughts" essays, to bring the esoteric class lessons to new places and other anthroposophical work groups, and to make the karma lectures more widely known; all these endeavors were steps on the way to gradually rooting the genuine change, which Rudolf Steiner had intended to initiate with the Christmas Conference, as an active force within the Anthroposophical Society. As she met with bitter resistance, particularly in Dornach, she withdrew increasingly to her own area of work.

In a meeting in May 1933, she said she would like to see the Clinical–Therapeutic Institute in Arlesheim as an anthroposophical work community, where all the leading personalities, in the hospital as well as in the center for curative education, the *Sonnenhof,* were actively involved. She added that she wished for more intensive anthroposophical basic studies and a repeated impulse for the active reception of Anthroposophy; she knew that this had been Rudolf Steiner's intention and that he had mentioned it repeatedly around the time of the Christmas Conference. Anthroposophy, as she said in Arlesheim and elsewhere, contained the substance of future cultural eras. There was, however, a real danger of a gradual spiritual decline at the Goetheanum, of Anthroposophy losing its radiant power, of its becoming diluted and distorted: "We must stand together so that Rudolf Steiner's ideas are not suddenly overthrown or even buried altogether. We must spread its seeds all over the world now so that the anthroposophical life can blossom everywhere.... What we are doing here is aimed at enhancing our connection with Rudolf Steiner. Despite all the difficulties that are rife in the Society we strive for the cohesion that is vital to our existence and work."[82]

In the early 1930s, Ita Wegman was determined to continue her efforts in and with the Anthroposophical Society, although she found this increasingly difficult: "*One really needs a great amount of energy to stop the incredible waves of hatred and misunderstanding being sent toward us and to resist them.*"[83] But she did not stop seeing the importance of a globally active Anthroposophical Society as a vessel for the School for Spiritual Science and as an esoteric community organ with an important spiritual task. Ita Wegman found that an efficiently working, transnational Anthroposophical Society was immensely important, particularly in view of the international political situation.

The Society's task was to maintain and actively represent the true image of the human being that was threatened by oppositional forces, to offer spiritual resistance, and to hold a protective hand over all the institutions that worked out of anthroposophical and humanitarian ideas—in education, curative education, medicine, social work, agriculture, and the arts. "It is quite obvious that the situation in the world has deteriorated massively with the failure of the Anthroposophical Society," she wrote to Lili Kolisko.[84] And yet, for a long time she did not give up the hope that the Anthroposophical Society would rally—maybe even because of the grim and increasingly dramatic international situation—and that it would let itself be inspired by the Christmas Conference. Fifteen years later, when nothing had changed, either in Dornach or at other centers of the Society, she encouraged some individuals—including Marie Steiner-von Sivers—to approach Anthroposophy in a more liberal way, outside the constraints and hindrances of the Anthroposophical Society. "Where the forms given by Doctor Steiner can no longer prevail, I for one support a liberal anthroposophical movement that will ignore the Society because this Society, as it appears now, will be incapable of spiritual growth," she wrote in 1931.[85]

Five years earlier she had written in a sympathetic and kind letter to a member in Silesia who had left the Anthroposophical Society, "It is with much regret that I read in your letter that the difficulties you met were so great that you felt you had to leave the Society. I do hope very much that this is a temporary situation and that you will be able to inform us soon that all these difficulties have been overcome. You can rest assured that we will continue to consider you as someone who belongs to us in principle. The world does, after all, not consist of members of the Anthroposophical Society alone, and anyone wishing to work with and embrace Anthroposophy in the right way will always find like-minded people."[86] *Someone who belongs to us*, Ita Wegman wrote, demonstrating the degree of broadmindedness that would be required in future. Nine years later the crisis in the Society reached its climax and on February 22,

1935, her fifty-ninth birthday, Ita Wegman wrote to Maria Röschl in a personal letter, "The [Anthroposophical] Society is no longer needed, because Anthroposophy has arrived on Earth. Every single person is important now and, together, we need to form a higher unity, which is rooted in the spiritual world. Individual developments will be respected; each person is free and can, out of his or her individual insight, feel connected with others in this spiritual association or Michael School."[87]

After the exclusions of the 1935 Annual General Meeting, Ita Wegman, helped by leading anthroposophists in Germany, Britain, and Holland, prevented—by withholding her active support—the formation of a second Anthroposophical Society and therefore the irrevocable division of the movement. She pointed out at various occasions that not the creation of new structures, but the intensified study of Anthroposophy and continued spiritual development of individuals would ensure future viability. "That way we will not form a [new] Society but a spiritual bond that will extend across all countries, [a bond] that is no earthly structure but a spiritual force."[88]

For Ita Wegman, the (new) Anthroposophical Society Rudolf Steiner initiated by laying a foundation stone in Dornach on December 25, 1923, was the only valid one, even if it had always been under a dark cloud. She hoped that more intensive basic studies of Anthroposophy and the continuation of the esoteric work of the First Class would bring about a process of transformation *within* the Society. The new spirit, she emphasized, always needed the old, was concerned with the latter's existence and further development and effected these in an ongoing process. "We can see ourselves, in the old Society, as the leaven and take the liberty we are spiritually justified in taking—but no more. We clearly have an even greater obligation now to deepen Anthroposophy; it is an inner law with each of us."[89]

In June 1938 she wrote to Eugen Kolisko* in London, advising him to keep his work in England as close to the Anthroposophical Society as possible. She added, "Dear Mr. Kolisko, you may laugh and say, 'I don't want anything further to do with the Anthroposophical Society,' and you may want to create something entirely different and unconnected with the Society. I believe, however, that we *are* part of this Society through Dr. Steiner and that we should gradually transform it. The aim of this metamorphosis should be that people work together loosely, while the Anthroposophical Society is there as a wider community: a community of new Christians who are willing to receive the resurrected Christ as a reality. This does not need to be said in so many words, but we need to bear it in our hearts. Only then will we achieve true spiritual successes."[90] She herself and many others were connected, in the way outlined by her, with the Anthroposophical Society and the Christmas Conference, *through Rudolf Steiner* and independently of the present leadership at the Goetheanum, and its views and decisions.

Ita Wegman wrote important letters and had crucial conversations; but how did she deal inwardly with the whole situation? In looking back she said that she decided to remain faithful in her heart to the intentions Rudolf

* Eugen Kolisko and his wife Lili were among the most eminent personalities within the Anthroposophical Society, and although Rudolf Steiner held them in high esteem they were increasingly marginalized after 1925 and driven into exile.

Steiner had pursued at the Christmas Conference, "unperturbed by anything else."[91] She always tried not to harbor illusions, mourn after things that were now impossible or "go on complaining without doing anything myself."[92] She had to make certain decisions for herself that allowed her to continue her work.

> One day I realized that I had to go back to the *basic impulse* Rudolf Steiner intended to give to the new Society by bringing down the teachings of Michael more than before from the Michaelic School in the spiritual world. I have heard much about this school from Rudolf Steiner, also about my and his relationship with it. To this impulse as the essence of the Christmas Conference I wish to return. I want to connect deeply with this impulse and work out of it. What will come of it I cannot yet say; I prepare myself and wait; I do not want to push myself to the fore, nor do I wish to commit myself. If there is something good in this impulse and if people come together who can be enthusiastic about this impulse, it will grow. It carries a future seed and it is the last thing Rudolf Steiner has entrusted to an earthly human being....[93] I am duty-bound to this Michael School and this duty will inform my actions and responsibilities. I wish to re-awaken awareness of this spirit association that exists in the spiritual world.[94]

During the course of 1934 and 1935, in the wake of a period of severe and almost fatal illness and crisis, as well as a journey to Palestine, Ita Wegman decided to let the chaotic situation in the Anthroposophical Society take its course and to focus instead (aside from her work in medicine and curative education) on the First Class, for which she bore special responsibility.[95] She hoped that one day the Anthroposophical Society would be re-formed out of the esoteric school and training, out of its esoteric roots. "Until that happens we need to work slowly, very slowly—this can probably only happen within people's hearts—on rebuilding this vessel in its pure form."[96] In a calm, benevolent, and positive spirit, she noted the withdrawals (about which she was told) from the medical field and curative education in the Society.

On September 9, 1941, she wrote to Helen Eugster, who worked at the *Sonnenhof:* "I have thought for some time now that we should free ourselves from the Society. It is no longer appropriate. We have to try and find new forms of implementing Rudolf Steiner's teachings."[97] As late as January 13, 1943, less than two months before her death, she wrote in a letter to the Arlesheim curative teacher Werner Pache, "I was interested to hear that you have left the Anthroposophical Society. I have heard of many young people who have done the same. Maybe the Society needs to be disbanded after all."[98]

Ita Wegman wrote "maybe"—she was not very sure herself. The painter Liane Collot d'Herbois, who was very close to her in her final years and lived with her in Ascona, near Casa Andrea Cristoforo, spoke later of how much Ita Wegman was preoccupied right to the end with the Goetheanum and the General Anthroposophical Society. "Dr. Wegman attributed the situation in the world largely to the situation within the Society. She said to me, *'If the three parts of the Society cannot come together, the whole war will have been in vain.'*"[99] According to Collot d'Herbois, Ita Wegman foresaw the end of the war and was constantly thinking about how this war could be transformed into something constructive. She thought that a continued division of the Society could only end in disaster. The Goetheanum—the "heart of the Society"—should, in her view, be seen as a group of people who were actively interested in the spiritual world. "If human beings, as the bearers of spiritual impulses, work together with united forces, they could have a harmonizing effect on the whole world."[100]

In mid-February 1943, two weeks before her death, Ita Wegman responded to Marie Steiner-von Sivers' call for reconciliation in the Dornach newsletter: "Your article is being interpreted in so many different ways. I will refrain from forming any judgement. I'm writing this letter merely to say that your words have made a deep impression on me; they are generous and forward-looking." Ita Wegman thanked Marie Steiner-von Sivers for her words and appeal, although various people pointed out to her that this call for reconciliation was by no means aimed at her. "Yet, from her words a hand stretches out toward me, and I would incur guilt if I did not take it."[101]

Eight years earlier, Ita Wegman had said in a letter that, even if the intentions of the Christmas Conference could not be implemented in the Society in its present condition ("the Christmas Conference as a whole is no longer functional..."[102]), the fact remained that the members of the Original Council were connected with Rudolf Steiner through an "act." They were therefore obliged "to work within the Anthroposophical Society and take responsibility for this work. If each of them does this work rightly, as intended by Rudolf Steiner, and if all those who are karmically connected with this work, join in and take proper care that everything unfolds in the right way, then the day will come, despite all difficulties, when we will be united again—even if that will only be in a future life."[103] Elsewhere she wrote, "*May one day the objective love hold sway in the*

Anthroposophical Society that we need so urgently if we are to take Rudolf Steiner's work forward in the right way."[104]

Like Marie Steiner-von Sivers, Ita Wegman never sought harmony or a contented Society for her own sake. The Anthroposophical Society and the esoteric Michael movement were, in her view, a community actively opposed to evil. She experienced and recognized the demons that were working against Michael, and she knew how the powers of Asuras and Sorat (and certainly not "only" Ahriman and Lucifer) were at work in the destructive work of fascism—and how they were manifest also in the breaking up of anthroposophical work groups and networks. Faced with this situation, she continued on her own inner way. When she was finally excluded from the Executive Council of the Anthroposophical Society in Dornach, she wrote in a letter to France on April 10, 1935, "Spiritual beings need nourishment, spiritual nourishment, which only human souls can give them. This nourishment grows from a particular inner attitude that is born from selflessness. If the souls can say 'yes' to the difficult trials they are facing, something good can come of that for the future. I think that is the test we need to pass, and on which much will depend in future."[105]

While little is known of Elisabeth Vreede's inner life, or her inner relationship with what Rudolf Steiner called the "Anthroposophical Society," we know even less of Guenther Wachsmuth, although he worked untiringly for the Society and the Goetheanum right up until 1963. Waldemar Kumm told me how he had destroyed Wachsmuth's personal estate at the latter's request. He spoke of his love for Guenther Wachsmuth and that others at the Goetheanum felt the same. The next generation, on the other hand, has found it difficult to relate to him, his role, and his inner intentions within the developing Anthroposophical Society—despite his correspondence with members and books that have been preserved in the Goetheanum's Documentation Department, and despite the biographies by Heinz-Herbert Schöffler, Uwe Werner, and others. In his comprehensive biography of Rudolf Steiner, Wachsmuth also held back with his personal views. "Such events are not for us to interpret; they are merely accessible to our experience. A connection with the event of the 1923 Christmas Conference must therefore arise in each individual soul...," he wrote in his characteristic way about Rudolf Steiner laying the Foundation Stone on December 25, 1924—"in each individual soul."[106]

When the first Goetheanum was inaugurated in October 1920, Guenther Wachsmuth was only twenty-three years old and was deeply impressed by this event. Rudolf Steiner had said one year earlier, "Without being immodest, one needs to see this building in Dornach really as the starting point of a great global and entirely international movement that encompasses all areas of the spiritual life."[107]

Guenther Wachsmuth joined the Anthroposophical Society in 1919, when he first visited Rudolf Steiner. Nine months later he was in the main auditorium attending the opening weeks of the School for Spiritual Science.

> The image of that moment is forever engraved in my memory: we awaited events while enjoying a musical prelude for organ and orchestra. The solemn and festive mood of a thousand people gathered in this auditorium for the first time; the huge sculpted columns that grow organically toward the painted dome of the ceiling; the light streaming in through the beautifully formed tall windows, bathing

> this world of sculptural forms in brilliant colors; a sublime *harmony* surrounded the expectant audience like a living being. All this was pervaded by a pulsating flow of receiving and giving, exchanged between each individual visitor and the building, like a life-giving first breath in the moment of birth. And in this *House of the Word* that exemplifies the intimate connection between the spiritual power active in it and its outer expression in the sculpted forms Rudolf Steiner now spoke to us for the first time.[108]

The opening address ended with the verse "*To turn to the light / in dark times of need,*"[109] and the "life-giving first breath in the moment of birth" would inspire Guenther Wachsmuth's anthroposophical biography until his death in March 1963. He was devoted fully to the General Anthroposophical Society as a global community of individuals to whom the *House of the Word* had been handed over and entrusted. At Guenther Wachsmuth's cremation in Basel, Albert Steffen said, "He heard Rudolf Steiner's lectures on the synthesis of the arts, sciences, and religion through spirit knowledge that, for him, culminated in a cosmic Christianity. And he resolved in that moment that he would devote his life to this spiritual impulse."[110] Directly after the opening of the Goetheanum, Guenther Wachsmuth declared in *Zeitschrift für soziale Dreigliederung*, the journal for social threefolding, "*Spiritual Science has initiated a new phase in its active striving for an ascending evolution of humanity.*"[111]

Guenther Wachsmuth learned in the years to come how critical Rudolf Steiner had been of many anthroposophical lectures given during the opening celebrations and how unhappy he had been about the "*mixtum compositum*" of Anthroposophy and conventional science presented there. Yet, when he looked back in 1941, Steiner pointed out, "But [the opening of the Goetheanum and the Dornach study weeks (*Hochschulwochen*)] set a goal to which each of us could aspire in the following years according to our individual 'gifts.'"[112] And this he did—invest all his "gifts," including his characteristic strength of will. Only six months after the opening of the Goetheanum he settled permanently in Dornach where he went on to work for the Anthroposophical Society, the Goetheanum, and the School for Spiritual Science for forty-two years, taking on a leading role from May 1921. Despite his youth he was promoted, when Roman Boos fell ill, to the position of Rudolf Steiner's secretary, acting as organizer and coordinator for him and the Society. He grew into these tasks incredibly quickly. According to Wachsmuth, Rudolf Steiner exuded "an atmosphere of calm and serenity, courage and steadfastness, inner focus and self-control"; from conversations with him one emerged feeling "inwardly calm, steady, grateful, ready to take action."[113] For almost four years Guenther Wachsmuth experienced Rudolf Steiner's work up close. He received quick, precise guidelines for answering incoming letters and witnessed personally Steiner's astounding ability to make a wide range of decisions quickly and with extraordinary concentration. This unique apprenticeship and training needs to be understood in depth by anyone seeking to understand Wachsmuth himself.

Beginning in April 1923, he also accompanied Rudolf Steiner on numerous journeys—to St. Gallen, Penmaenmawr, Tintagel, Prague, Wroclaw, Kobierzyce, Weimar, Vienna, and many other places. Steiner climbed with Wachsmuth to the stone circles on the plateau above Penmaenmawr and explained them to him. He showed him Weimar, spent time with him in book shops in Prague and with Rosa Mayreder in Vienna. On the train from Vienna to Basel, he even organized a small, impromptu party for Wachsmuth's thirtieth birthday, as well as many similar attentions, all in a charming and original way. Once, when they were in a restaurant and Wachsmuth started eating his double portion of spaghetti, Steiner sat silently next to him, leaving his own food untouched. He said after a while, *"That's some ether body you have!"*[114]

"Occupation: secretary," it said in an official document. In February 1923, this "secretary," on behalf of Rudolf Steiner, gave Emil Bock the ritual text for the appointment of the *Erzoberlenker* (head) of the Christian Community, and he represented Steiner when Friedrich Rittelmeyer was ordained into this office. Steiner had read the words personally to Guenther Wachsmuth before asking him to pass them on to Emil Bock and Friedrich Rittelmeyer.

> I shall never forget the moment when Rudolf Steiner asked me to listen to the ritual first before he handed me this momentous document on his sickbed, below the Christ Statue. In a voice that had grown gentle and soft from illness, but forming the words with great feeling and spirit, he read out the serene text of the Act of Ordination. Only in such rare, essential moments did I experience Rudolf Steiner so inwardly moved and at the same time elated by the act carried out. When he had read the words he handed them to me, saying, *"This is given directly from the spiritual world."*[115]

Except for personal or private letters, Guenther Wachsmuth also answered all of Rudolf Steiner's correspondence until the end. The office had been moved *into* the Goetheanum (from Haus Friedwart), because it was Steiner's wish that letters be delivered to and answered from that building to imbue them with the true "spirit of the Goetheanum."[116]

At Guenther Wachsmuth's cremation, Albert Steffen spoke of him as Steiner's secretary: "Rudolf Steiner was most satisfied with this ideal colleague. He was delighted with Guenther Wachsmuth's enthusiastic nature, even with this tempo—with the constant looking toward the future."[117] At the Goetheanum and in the Anthroposophical Society, Steffen spoke of Wachsmuth's particular temperament, which made him the "ideal colleague." He described Wachsmuth as "enthusiastic" and dwelled on his dynamic, forward-looking disposition. Indeed, Wachsmuth had an open and cheerful personality; he was extremely versatile and sanguine, walked with an optimistic spring in his step, and exuded "radiance and inspiration." Albert Steffen spoke highly of Wachsmuth's "freshness and verve," emphasizing that it was not merely the expression of a pleasant temperament, but also a quality that emanated "from the higher self in him."[118]

According to Albert Steffen, Wachsmuth's "spirit-filled energy" and "natural unforced politeness"[119] made him the ideal secretary and travel companion for Rudolf Steiner. He spoke several languages, was never chatty, and had style, strength, and sparkling buoyancy. Both during and after Rudolf Steiner's lifetime, many people directly experienced Wachsmuth's qualities at the Goetheanum, combined with the inner reserve, or even reticence, that characterized him. He worked tirelessly and selflessly for the Anthroposophical Society. Letters from members were answered promptly, and his immediate and highly valued colleagues at the Goetheanum were kept up to date with developments and decisions at the Goetheanum and in the Society in the hope of their "united support."[120] The deep respect for Rudolf Steiner's intentions were always tangible and continued to be binding for Wachsmuth.

Rudolf Steiner once spoke to Edith Maryon of Guenther Wachsmuth as an "all-arounder." His experience, after 1921, of Steiner's increasingly challenging and tragic struggle for the Anthroposophical Society caused a change in Wachsmuth; earnestness began to permeate his being and work, as well as an extraordinary reliability in all he did for the Goetheanum and the Anthroposophical Society. He never forgot how alone Rudolf Steiner had been in his concern for the future of the Goetheanum. This experience also formed the basis for his absolute devotion to "the Dornach cause," or "the Doctor's cause," as Andrei Bely once put it. From the very beginning, Wachsmuth was involved actively in the initiatives to rebuild the Goetheanum after the fire. Thanks to his personal commitment, a positive decision was reached at the international conference of delegates in July 1923. The initiative for this gathering for the reconstruction of the Goetheanum came from the Anthroposophical Society in Switzerland, which was then joined by the Society in England.

In Switzerland, Albert Steffen and Guenther Wachsmuth were instrumental in those events—the General Secretary of the Swiss Society and his secretary, a position accepted by Wachsmuth in April 1923 at Steffen's request. Wachsmuth was responsible for the (international) correspondence and met many people. At the annual meeting of the Anthroposophical Society in Switzerland, he pleaded for a greater sense of community and referred to building a new Goetheanum as the greatest task of the Swiss Anthroposophical Society. He chaired the crucial meetings at the international conference of delegates and urged the individual countries to firmly commit to the financial support they had promised. He also stipulated that Rudolf Steiner should have full freedom of financial disposition and action. In a conversation with Guenther Wachsmuth in the fall of 1923, Steiner said he would not lay a new foundation stone for the building, because the first stone retained its full spiritual effectiveness and continuity. "Nonetheless, I will add a different kind of foundation stone."[121]

At the Christmas Conference for the new foundation of the Anthroposophical Society and its School for Spiritual Science, Rudolf Steiner made Guenther Wachsmuth a member of the Executive Council at the young age of thirty years, which surprised many. According to Steiner, Wachsmuth would spare this group (and himself) many worries, think for all of them, and "keep their heads together." Wachsmuth was allowed to recite the new bylaws at the meeting, and Steiner would later offer him a gift of his handwritten draft. For nearly four decades, Wachsmuth was treasurer of both the Goetheanum and the General Anthroposophical Society. During his illness, Rudolf Steiner often asked, "How is it going with the building, Wachsmuth?" Until his own death in the spring of 1963, Wachsmuth would never forget this. It profoundly informed his work ethic in Dornach.

On March 5, 1925, just four weeks before his death, Rudolf Steiner wrote to Marie Steiner-von Sivers in Berlin from his studio in Dornach: "Things are going very slowly with me, and I *have to* be ready to work soon. After everything that has been going on, it is inconceivable what might happen if the building work were disrupted because of my illness."[122]

Guenther Wachsmuth knelt at Rudolf Steiner's deathbed, and later he wrote about the passing of the great teacher:

> When he breathed his last, [Rudolf Steiner] himself closed his eyes. No sense of finality filled the room, but rather one of enhanced spiritual activity. A serene, transfigured wakefulness was reflected in his countenance, in the praying gesture of his hands. Just as great artists of the past made recumbent medieval knights on their sarcophagi look as if their closed eyes could still see, their resting bodies still striding forth, likewise the resting figure here spoke of an unearthly wakefulness, striding forth into spheres of the spirit.[123]

"Striding forth" on Earth with the Goetheanum, the General Anthroposophical Society, and the School for Spiritual Science in Dornach was what Guenther Wachsmuth intended to do from then on, despite all the difficulties that gradually unfolded. He repeatedly pointed out, "A global movement such as ours" should be able to do that.[124] Rudolf Steiner's words about continuing to build the Goetheanum became an inner obligation for him, an absolute and unchangeable necessity.

As early as 1926 and 1927, he (and Jan Stuten), armed with two photographs of the second Goetheanum, traveled around Europe visiting the anthroposophic groups in various countries to raise funds to complete the building. He even had his address given in Hamburg in May 1926 printed. Among other things, he had spoken of the connection between the two foundation stones, the spiritual and the physical, concluding with reference to Steiner's anxious question in his final hours about the building and its progress ("How is it going with the building, Wachsmuth?"). A year after Steiner's death he said,

> We will find ourselves confronted by this big question day after day until we have acted on it: How is it going with the building? As long as we fail to complete what he has brought down for us from the spiritual world as his last deed, what has become a reality in his model, we will not find inner peace. We must answer the question posed to us, "How is it going with the building?" as soon as we possibly can by saying, "The building is finished!"...We must make this possible, dear friends; we must open the Goetheanum next year so that we can provide an answer to the spiritual world.[125]

Despite all efforts, the second Goetheanum was not opened in 1927, but a year later at Michaelmas 1928, as 2,600 people gathered to celebrate the occasion. Rudolf Steiner's first and second mystery dramas were performed and lectures held in the main auditorium and carpentry shop. Guenther Wachsmuth was thirty-five at the time and in charge of the organization. He gave an important lecture (Oct. 2, 1928), entitled "The Word Reveals Itself in Nature." Four days later, the performances and main lectures of the conference had to be repeated, and between those events Wachsmuth celebrated his thirty-fifth birthday on October 4.

Guenther Wachsmuth's main concern after 1928—as the global economic crisis came to a head and totalitarian regimes sprung up across Europe—was to preserve the

Goetheanum as the home of the General Anthroposophical Society and the School for Spiritual Science. Against this background, he tried to expand the circles that supported the Goetheanum (economically).

In 1934, one year after the Nazis seized power in Germany, he went to the United States for two months, where he gave more than a hundred talks, speaking of the cultural significance of the Anthroposophical Society and the Goetheanum building.

Seven years later, in 1941, partly as a result of his efforts, thirty-seven percent of the Goetheanum's income came from the U.S. This meant that the building continued to exist and function, albeit with reduced capacity, despite the losses resulting from the ban on the German Society, which had so far supplied most of the members and finances. "*We promise that we will continue the work whatever happens,*" Wachsmuth wrote to the members in early 1940, just six months after the beginning of World War II.[126] To drastically reduce all heating costs and overhead, he moved all activities, including the mystery dramas, to the carpentry, while Swiss soldiers were temporarily billeted in the Goetheanum building. Marie Steiner-von Sivers made sure that Rudolf Steiner's written estate was taken to a safe place far away from Dornach. While the carpentry shop evoked intense memories of Rudolf Steiner in him, Guenther Wachsmuth continued to focus on the future. Rudolf Grosse later recalled that, during the difficult war years, Wachsmuth spoke of three remaining tasks for which he felt personally responsible: the extension of the main auditorium; the preservation of the studio and the carpentry shop (where the new foundation of the General

Anthroposophical Society had been enacted in 1923/24); and the opening of the west entrance.[127]

Even during the World War, Guenther Wachsmuth's duties included more than being an organizer and treasurer. In 1941, he published the first history of Rudolf Steiner's life and work (*The Life and Work of Rudolf Steiner: From the Turn of the Century to His Death*), a tome of more than 600 pages. He had taken on this project reluctantly; he had never seen himself as a biographer, and he was fully aware of the responsibility that such a document demanded. He saw the danger that the originator of Anthroposophy would be forgotten over time or concealed or misinterpreted by future generations.

A year later, in 1942, he published the most extensive and detailed bibliography of Rudolf Steiner's work at the time. After Wachsmuth's death on March 4, 1963, Carl Jacob Burckhardt wrote to Albert Steffen about how deeply impressed he was with Wachsmuth's "steady inner growth."[128] Burckhardt attended the cremation ceremony for his former roommate from Glarisegg.[129] With Guenther Wachsmuth, this "steady inner growth" was always interwoven with his spiritual work.

It was a surprise to many that Guenther Wachsmuth's work after 1921 or '22 was essentially in the area of natural science. He was an erudite man who had attended excellent schools in Switzerland and Germany (Glarisegg, Wickersdorf, and Langensalza). Later he studied law, constitutional law, economics, and international politics at various universities, including Oxford. He considered a diplomatic career and wrote his doctoral dissertation on communication and media in international law, but then he went to Dornach, where he began working with the scientist Ehrenfried Pfeiffer on research into "etheric forces." Wachsmuth and Pfeiffer manufactured the first biodynamic preparations for a new approach to farming with a process inspired and accompanied by Rudolf Steiner. He had told Albert Steffen, "I will create a special field of work for Guenther Wachsmuth."[130]

In the early 1920s, Guenther Wachsmuth had started to study the "Earth's breathing" and etheric geography. Rudolf Steiner was overjoyed and gave him the opportunity to speak about the "face of the Earth and the destiny of humanity" at the Christmas Conference. Steiner had originally planned to give Wachsmuth the Goetheanum sections for economics and social science but then, as it turned out, was greatly satisfied with his "fruitful" natural-scientific work. He closely supervised Wachsmuth's manuscript for *Etheric Formative Forces in Cosmos, Earth, and Man,* of which 3,000 copies were printed in 1924, bearing Steiner's picture on the cover. This monograph was greatly appreciated by anthroposophically oriented medical students and physicians, farmers who had attended the course at Koberwitz, priests of The Christian Community, and artists. It became one of the most successful books of the anthroposophical movement following the Christmas Conference, and Guenther Wachsmuth continued to work on many of the topics addressed in this book, despite his manifold other commitments. He worked as industriously on biology and the earth sciences as he did on the history of humanity and consciousness.

In 1945, Guenther Wachsmuth's outstanding work on the formative forces, rhythms, and life processes of the

Earth and humanity was published (*Erde und Mensch: ihre Bildekräfte, Rhythmen und Lebensprozesse*), in which he presented the Earth as a living organism, taking into account all the relevant scientific knowledge of his time. No monograph published by the Goetheanum has seen such a positive reception and reviews from non-anthroposophic circles (including the Swiss medical weekly journal *Schweizer Medizinische Wochenschrift*). Wachsmuth recognized early on how important modern research into rhythms was and published an impressive overview that included a biometeorology of the nature realms. Gaining in-depth insights into the natural rhythms would provide the key to the true science of nature, Rudolf Steiner had once said;[131] and Guenther Wachsmuth presented a remarkable synopsis on the subject. Albert Steffen spoke later of Wachsmuth's "*cosmic insights*,"[132] and was not the only one wondering where all this knowledge came from. Many people were struck at how topical Wachsmuth's work was, and how significant in the cultural and economic crisis of that time—and he did not hold back with his views.

In October 1957, Wachsmuth spoke out against the launch of Sputnik, which he saw as an "unscrupulous use of [artificial] Earth satellites, which would harm the most delicate organic systems in the human body."[133] Instead of studying and exploiting space technology, one should strive to continue Goethe's approach and acquire a deeper understanding of the biology and ecology of the earthly organism as a whole. Goethe had said to Eckermann on October 7, 1827, "We all wander among mysteries. We are surrounded by an atmosphere and do not yet know what lives in it and how it relates to our spirit."[134]

For Guenther Wachsmuth (as a student of Rudolf Steiner), the Earth is an ensouled and spirit-imbued mortal being that contains the seed of resurrection. He felt strongly that this fact needed to be made known in all its details before it was too late. At the cremation ceremony for Guenther Wachsmuth, Albert Steffen said, "He started from the cosmos. He never really mentioned this, but he was still pervaded by the impulses of the ancient Egyptian and Persian mysteries. As it was for Plato, the Sun was a divine being for Wachsmuth—*sol invictus*, the unconquered Sun, which bowed to the Earth and became part of it through the Mystery of Golgotha. From that moment, the Earth was changed; it became radiant, bearing a spiritual light within. He explored that radiance."[135] He changed from (constitutional) law to natural science, but never neglected the arts. When Albert Steffen first met Wachsmuth in Munich, he was playing music by Handel. Later, he had his own organ in his house in Dornach. He wrote several plays, which Albert Steffen greatly appreciated and performed at the Goetheanum. According to Steffen, Wachsmuth was a born artist who had sacrificed his artistic gifts and goals mostly (though not entirely) to his work in and around the Anthroposophical Society.

Wachsmuth was always intensely aware of the General Anthroposophical Society and its "sublime" building in Dornach. He was a modern individual, who had a radio and television in his private home. Nevertheless, he was strictly against installing electricity and telephones throughout the Goetheanum, because he found that human encounters there are so important. He said it is crucial to be aware of the Goetheanum in its entirety and not to deliver it into the fangs and tricks of Ahriman. He was always conscious of the building's dedication and purpose, and despite his personal love of music he did not agree to the organization of large concerts at the Goetheanum. People could go to Basel for concerts, he said. The Goetheanum had more specific tasks, including the development and performance of the new mystery art of eurythmy. "Tasks, tasks, tasks," were Wachsmuth's last words to Albert Steffen.[136]

> I was united in You.
> Remain united in me.
> We will speak together
> In the language of eternal being.
> We will be active
> Where deeds take effect,
> We will weave in spirit
> Where human thoughts are woven
> In the word of eternal thought.[137]

These lines by Rudolf Steiner were read at Guenther Wachsmuth's cremation. Albert Steffen wrote a poem for his colleague and friend, "In Memory of Guenther Wachsmuth," which describes the despair felt at the threatening destruction of the Earth, though it ends on a more poetic note:

> The dead now approaches,
> whom in life we loved as a seeker of truth,
> and he speaks to my soul, "Behold the life within you,
> the breath moved by the wandering stars,
> your heartbeat flooded with Sun's own light,
> wherein a window opens to the immortal Self,
> of visions left behind on Earth."

In memory of Guenther Wachsmuth, Albert Steffen wrote of the resurrection of creation, the minerals, the plants, and the bees. He wrote about Mother Nature and her mercy toward us as human beings who are destroying the Earth, about our turning to the hierarchy of love, and about the resurrection of the "I." Steffen considered Wachsmuth to be a person concerned with and actively committed to "*Natura*"—in the heart of the Anthroposophical Society and in the Society's "building of truth" in Dornach.

Albert Steffen found the Anthroposophical Society difficult from the beginning and had to work to overcome antipathy. Steffen was only twenty-two when he encountered Rudolf Steiner and Anthroposophy in Berlin, where he attended a lecture on human biography. "*I gave to you the strength of truth. / If it enkindles its fiery might in you, / then you will find the way.*"[138] Steffen found his way, but he was not looking for community—not even the community of those who gathered around Rudolf Steiner and Anthroposophy. They were, and remained, alien to him. They seemed to him at first like a "wall" around the spiritual teacher; as a true artist, he felt he was in the wrong place and resolutely rejected the thought of becoming a member. "Whenever I spoke of this with others, I say 'No!' as well as when I hear of their adulation of Rudolf Steiner, how these people speak about their advancement, or when I see their faces."[139] He deeply felt the discrepancy between Steiner's "purest spirit will" and the "clumsiness" of his students, and he wished to keep his distance: "*I prefer to be by myself.*"[140]

When he saw the mystery dramas performed in Munich, he realized how difficult and how necessary it was to build a spiritual community and decided, in 1910, after three years of anthroposophical studies and a personal conversation with Rudolf Steiner, to take the step of joining the

Society. Many years later, the building in Dornach profoundly impressed him. "Its forms are taken from cosmic evolution; they have a widening, liberating, exhilarating, and conciliating effect; they imbue us with divine love."[141] The growing Johannes Building became a "mighty and gentle" friend to him; its forms have the power to disperse painful memories and make great goals light up. In joining the work, Steffen felt new life arising in the shared (community-building) "love for the work," and he sensed the tasks that awaited humanity in the heart of Europe—tasks connected with this building: *"I saw that they were recognized and reached for at the Goetheanum."*[142]

Rudolf Steiner spoke of "building the anthroposophical cause" and about the educational purpose of the joint undertaking begun in Dornach. Albert Steffen experienced the building as an actual "guide to the higher Self" of the individual and community. In the summer of 1914, he went to the Goetheanum for the first time to help with the work.

In 1920, at the age of thirty-five, Albert Steffen returned ready to stay for good: "I am willing to take destiny upon myself."[143] Once in Dornach, Steffen soon realized the kind of burden Rudolf Steiner had to bear alone ("He is a cross-bearer").[144] He also heard Steiner speak at the Goetheanum after the autumn of 1920 and was deeply moved by what he heard in this earthly "home" of Anthroposophy. "I have never seen anyone like this—anyone as ageless and unburdened by his physical body as Rudolf Steiner was at the Goetheanum, where he was surrounded by the colors and forms he himself brought down from the world of gods."[145] "When Rudolf Steiner spoke from the lectern, everyone, whatever their country of origin, said to themselves, 'Yes, there is a spiritual home on Earth.'"[146]

At the first event of the School for Spiritual Science event to be held in Dornach, at the opening of the Goetheanum—the *Hochschulkurs* that changed Guenther Wachsmuth's life profoundly—Albert Steffen gave a talk, "Crises in the Artist's Life." He experienced many crises himself but took on more and more community tasks at the request of Rudolf Steiner, starting by becoming editor of the weekly *Das Goetheanum* in June 1921. He would edit this journal every week for more than forty-two years, for six times seven years, until July 1963, initially in cooperation with Rudolf Steiner. This work also brought home to him what Steiner really wanted to achieve with the Goetheanum building, the School for Spiritual Science, and the Anthroposophical Society, which was to carry and promote everything: "He foresaw a great mystery era."[147] Albert Steffen wrote down entire courses by Rudolf Steiner for the members and for the readers of the weekly journal as a way of cultivating a shared consciousness.

At Rudolf Steiner's request, in May 1922 Steffen also took on the challenge of becoming General Secretary of the Swiss Society, though he continued to see himself as a "wanderer." Together with Guenther Wachsmuth and "on behalf of the Anthroposophical Society in Switzerland," Steffen sent invitations for the Christmas Conference to members worldwide, and—at Rudolf Steiner's further request—agreed to give the opening lecture at this momentous event, speaking on "The Karmic History of the Goetheanum." Using emphatic words and images, he spoke of laying the Foundation Stone and the fire. Rudolf Steiner saw Steffen's introduction as *"a star"* that shone over the events of the following days.[148] In retrospect, Albert Steffen wrote of the Anthroposophical Society at the Christmas Conference:

> And to precisely this moment [of the laying of the Foundation Stone in 1913] he went back when he sank the Foundation Stone into the hearts of the members, when the hammer strokes resounded again, this time as heartbeats, and when he encapsulated the human situation in the words that form the foundation of our Society. These are not lifeless words: they are living forces, and just as architecture, painting, and music, all the arts, have grown from these words, so will everything grow from them that happens in this community.[149]

It was Rudolf Steiner's aim, and achievement, to inspire such spiritual community-building and global consciousness, using, among other things, the new Society newsletter *Was in der Anthroposophischen Gesellschaft vorgeht* (What is happening in the Anthroposophical Society). Steffen actively supported this endeavor in his own way with never-failing loyalty.

On New Year's Day 1925, Albert Steffen represented Rudolf Steiner (who was then seriously ill) in the carpentry shop, speaking of the cohesion within the Anthroposophical Society. He reminded his listeners of their shared attempts to put out the fire on the disastrous night of December 31, 1922, and the buckets of water they had passed from the carpentry shop to the Goetheanum's south entrance, which did not, however, stop the tremendous blaze and probably looked pointless if not pathetic from the outside. Yet, according to Albert Steffen, they created "an inner community that would never be lost."[150]

On Rudolf Steiner's last birthday on Earth, Albert Steffen gave another lecture in the carpentry shop, very close to the studio where Steiner lay on his sickbed. A request had gone out to all branches of the Anthroposophical Society worldwide, asking members to gather. Steffen referred to the Michael Imagination and the Foundation Stone Meditation and to Rudolf Steiner's mantric verses, which by that time (February 27, 1925) were already a legacy. He spoke of the need to renew the act of the Christmas Conference and the sense of community. Four weeks later, at Rudolf Steiner's cremation, he referred to the "friend of god and leader of humanity."

For Albert Steffen, the Anthroposophical Society he had joined—reluctantly at first—was an "invisible church" and the goal of the future age of the "spirit self" in the consciousness soul. For him, as an unwavering individualist, it was all about the intention of the spirit community, which combined the ideal of the "free spiritual life" with the power of "all-embracing love." "*Our home, however, is the truth / founded and lived in the spirit.*"[151] His devotion to Anthroposophy and to building a community based on Anthroposophy he saw increasingly as his contribution to preparing the age of the spirit self: the era when each human being will be acknowledged and loved as such, as "purely human" (Paracelsus).

Seen in this light, the Anthroposophical Society was an institution of the "public life" for Albert Steffen. Rudolf Steiner, he emphasized, had bequeathed Anthroposophy to all people—not just to a particular community that was pursuing its own interests. Rudolf Steiner was a bearer of the Christ impulse and his aim was to bring salvation to all humankind. Similarly, the Goetheanum was intended as a home for *all* people—a point Albert Steffen enlarged upon to great effect in Dornach on September 3, 1939, just after the beginning of World War II.[152] But Steffen was also certain that humankind was standing close to a real abyss. "The human being, created by the arbiters of the world, is in danger of destroying himself with his own 'I'-being," he wrote in his *Stiftungsdrama,* a play about the foundation of the Anthroposophical Society.[153] He had witnessed how, from 1914 onward, members of different nations, groups, and religions worked together to build the Goetheanum as a "work of peace" and a model of social cooperation. The fact "that, at a time when civilization broke down, a community of people felt united through the power of the spirit"[154] had made a deep and lasting impression on him, and he reminded his listeners of this experience in the early days of World War II. Anthroposophy is a force for peace, Albert Steffen said on September 3, 1939, that could transform humankind. Rudolf Steiner, during the Christmas Conference, had again appealed to anthroposophists and their willingness "to find spirit vision and the spiritual life through inner deepening."[155]

According to Albert Steffen, the Anthroposophical Society was about establishing, or reestablishing, a "site of the all-consuming sacrificial fire." The building work at the Goetheanum in the middle of World War I had united and strengthened the community, and this strength continued to shine out, as proof of what Anthroposophy was able to achieve within its "Society." Against this background, raising the Anthroposophical Society to the level of a "universally human" institution constituted a great and encouraging future goal and vision. "We must prepare ourselves for bringing something into the world once the 'war' is over." What would then be brought to the world needed to be spirit-imbued and sustainable, Steffen pointed out. "It is important that what we will provide complies with the requirements of the spiritual world."[156]

Albert Steffen often focused on the urgent needs of civilization, not only in his address of September 3, 1939, but also in his plays. He expected the Anthroposophical Society, as a spiritual community, to take an active interest in the contemporary spiritual, social, and political struggle of humanity. Rudolf Steiner had made it quite clear again at the Christmas Conference that the Anthroposophical Society had the task of propagating Anthroposophy and that it therefore needed to be aware of the questions, problems, and needs of the time: "We must take to heart what Rudolf Steiner said, '*Anthroposophy is here. It has been developed. I pledge to do all I can to make it known in the world.*'[157] These words in particular could be a meditation on how to enter into the matters of the Anthroposophical Society in the right way."[158]

According to Albert Steffen it falls to the Anthroposophical Society to "make known in the world" the spiritual research results of the School for Spiritual Science. It has to carry the spiritual achievements into today's civilization and culture and make them available to those who are looking out for them.

> Anthroposophy was already there when Rudolf Steiner edited Goethe's writings, but only as a germ. It became Spiritual Science. It became art. It became—society. It became a society akin to the essence of Anthroposophy when it was given form through the content itself, at the laying of

> the Foundation Stone. But here it was planted in the heart of each one and needs to be lived and developed by each one. It cannot be blamed on the living and indestructible being of Anthroposophy when branches on this tree turn dry and drop off. Individual branches can only ever heal if they reconnect, again and again, with the basic force: with the being that originates in the spiritual world. There is no remedy other than studying Anthroposophy at even greater depth and taking the Foundation Stone seriously—getting to know the writings better and better, from the first to the last, and practicing the methods for yourself. This will give you the strength to become active. It does not stand in the way of doing outer work but is rather a precondition *for it.* For all we can do is take Anthroposophy out there. "*It can only be a matter of telling the world what needs to be said from the anthroposophical center and wait and see how many people will understand it.*"[159] This is the route we will take. The initially small group will grow and emanate courage and joy. As long as this group works honestly it will succeed, even if the world around it is shaken and falling to pieces; for Anthroposophy has already passed through death; and the "pupils of spirit knowledge" receive their strength from suprasensory realms, from the experience of resurrection.[160]

In 1923, after the Goetheanum fire, Rudolf Steiner tried more than ever to instill in the members of the Anthroposophical Society an understanding of the great responsibility they had toward the living being of Anthroposophy. The small group of anthroposophists, he said at the time, had to be a "model" when it came to this responsibility. Seventeen years later, in 1940—during World War II—Albert Steffen began his *Stiftungsdrama* in an attempt to dramatize the history of the Anthroposophical Society after the laying of the Foundation Stone for the Johannes Building on September

20, 1913. Just before the act that depicts the laying of the foundation stone, Steffen shows Marie Steiner-von Sivers (the "life companion") in conversation with Rudolf Steiner: "Alone, left to yourself / you are a victor. But weighed down, as you are, / by the destiny of others / who fail to advance / it is a struggle. // *I am accustomed to such burden. Moreover / I shall help each one to find their inner strength* // I see the spirit-seekers gathered / divided and with adverse goals. / *The building will unite them.*" In this dramatic dialog Rudolf Steiner says of the cosmic cult and the future:

> I see a shining stream of helpers,
> pouring into the gloomy century
> that has just ended, and illumine it,
> when I behold the foundation stone of this edifice.
> To this I would call everyone's attention.
> How can discord live in any heart,
> when we find the sun home within us.[161]

In March 1942, on the occasion of Marie Steiner-von Sivers' seventy-fifth birthday, Albert Steffen read the scene "The day of the laying of the Foundation Stone" from his fragment *Stiftungsdrama* in the carpentry shop, despite—or because of—the discord and conflicts that had flared up. The "salvation of the Society" continued to be the ideal that guided him, because it was prerequisite to the Society's spiritual efficacy. Like all the other members of the original Council, Steffen was deeply affected by the Society's decline. "I was again filled with profound sadness. My heart can hardly bear it. And there is no hope of improvement," he wrote in his diary on March 24, 1942.[162] "*You are destined for the spirit / and yet you falter upon entering the grave? If only one would wash the other's wounds / that he inflicted.*

Go forth and say this: / How knowledge pointed you toward love."[163]

Elsewhere, Albert Steffen wrote of Rudolf Steiner, "It will always be good to look back to the past as one strides on, and to remember how the greatest person one has met in life mastered the problems of the community; and never forget all the same that he, too, suffered from them and gave his best forces for them—often in vain. Knowing this aspect of Rudolf Steiner's life will give us strength to bear the burden and maybe to persuade others to help us lighten the load."[164]

Fallow soil of stretching furrow,
Wintry damp and grave-like gloom
Has transformed into the bloom,
The white vessel of a flower.

Now its chalice and its crown
Become bright countenance and wings:
Christ lifts you from the hill and brings
You to the holiest empyrean.

How the choir of stars rings forth
And all the children of heaven aloft
Rejoice to see your earthly beauty lift
Gently away and free itself from death.

Yes, you come in earthly garment
But from all corruption free:
Henceforth angels will be glad to see
Human beings in spirit's firmament.

For now that you have cleansed the colors
Of the Earth, they love them well.
God with human is reconciled
By grace of your benevolent gesture.[165]

The benevolent gesture that marked Rudolf Steiner's earthly deeds in and outside of the Anthroposophical Society continued to be exemplary for Albert Steffen and his colleagues on the original Executive Council.

In the karma lectures we learn that this "benevolent gesture" was already effective in the cosmic cult of the Michael School. Rudolf Steiner described there how, in the early decades of the nineteenth century, the members of the Michael Community "celebrated" the teachings of the Michael School in cosmic images close to the Earth—in a cosmic-spiritual ceremony. This celebration was led by eminent personalities of the Michael Community, but the whole community was involved in "weaving" the cosmic imaginations. All this had a profound effect, even on the will of those who were involved, inspiring them to seek anthroposophical community-building in a future incarnation.

> Those who today feel the urge to unite within the Anthroposophical Society met in the nineteenth century in suprasensory regions to carry out the potent imaginative cult about which I have spoken....[166] Those who have the gift to recognize the souls now that they are incarnated will know that they worked together in the first half of the nineteenth century, when the mighty cosmic imaginations were placed into the suprasensory world, representing what I would call the "new Christianity."[167]

The Michael Community aspired to inaugurating the "new Christianity," or founding the new Christian Mysteries. Rudolf Steiner worked within that community, cosmically as well as on Earth. He envisaged the Anthroposophical Society as "resulting from the most profound human humility."[168] This society was to take spiritual truths seriously; its members were to erect a spiritual "building," founded on truth and successful self-education. This inner space, or esoteric essence, of the Anthroposophical Society was immensely precious to Rudolf Steiner. In this inner space, in the hearts of the members, Spiritual Science was to be further developed in thinking and feeling as a way of ensuring the "continuation of human existence." All individually gained anthroposophical insights, Rudolf Steiner once said, aim to ignite "human love:" human love that "teaches us about the value of being human and that allows us to experience human dignity."[169] At the opposite pole was the "destructive potential" of modern civilization of which Rudolf Steiner spoke very succinctly[170] at the conclusion of the Christmas Conference. This destructive potential would manifest in the following decades of the twentieth century as mass murder, genocide, euthanasia, and terror.

The Anthroposophical Society was to create an atmosphere where people could "breathe while educating themselves."[171] Rudolf Steiner emphasized repeatedly in 1923 that anthroposophists

> must not deny this center [of the Anthroposophical Society]; Waldorf teachers must not deny it; the staff of [the joint-stock company] *Der Kommende Tag* must not deny it, researchers and physicians must not deny it. They must not even dream of saying, "I have no time for general anthroposophical matters." Although each of these enterprises, in the case of such denial, would be able to survive for a while, because Anthroposophy is full of life and able to instill life, this life could not be maintained: it would eventually run dry and the enterprises in question would fail."[172]

According to Rudolf Steiner the Anthroposophical Society needs to create and maintain this inner space as well as be actively interested in the world's current concerns and needs. As early as 1907 he referred to the Anthroposophical Society (then the German Section of the Theosophical Society) as a core community from which the force for social renewal needed to radiate out. True social change, as he said then and later, could only arise from spiritual impulses, and it was important that Anthroposophy was represented from out of the anthroposophical center.

During the Christmas Conference, Rudolf Steiner again encouraged "the students of spirit knowledge" to internalize and follow the impulses from the spiritual world (which had first been conceived in the Michael School and in the Michaelic cult). In September 1913, when he laid the foundation stone for the Johannes Building, he had first spoken of the "spiritual fight" that needed to be waged by individuals "aglow with the fire of love."[173]

The "salutary sensation" of "not being adequate to the task," which Rudolf Steiner described in 1914 during the inauguration of the Glass House,[174] has affected many members of the Anthroposophical Society; it also affected the members of the original Council. This inadequacy also related to the lack of cohesion in the Society and the inability to work together.

During autumn 1923, Rudolf Steiner spoke in Vienna about the Michaelic championing of the truth of spiritual impulses, whether or not they could be implemented successfully. What was important was that people had confidence in the inner truth of the cause; spiritual truths had to become as real as the physical ground they walked on. The same applied to the inevitable failures to build a successful community and to the trust in the inner truth of spiritual *community impulses* that are not—and cannot—be lost. The aim of the Christmas Conference was to awaken in the members a shared awareness of the essence of the Anthroposophical Society and of Anthroposophy. The members of the Executive Council, who failed in the end, were also part of this membership. *"In order later to achieve the goal / of his own being, which he knows to lie / in the far distant future."*[175] These lines from the mystery drama were like a future promise to the members of the Society and their Executive Council, whose community-building on Earth had thus far not succeeded.

"We must seek to awaken in us the Sun force of Rudolf Steiner that shines out to us from the Representative of Humanity," Albert Steffen said on December 25, 1932, at the inauguration ceremony for the *Gruppenraum* (Group Room), where the statue is kept at the Goetheanum.[176] It is important, he continued, to give form and life, then and in the future, to the sacrifice Rudolf Steiner had made for the Anthroposophical Society ("How can discord live in any heart, / when we find the Sun home within us... ").[177] Elsewhere Steffen wrote,

> The Anthroposophical Society has become truly esoteric because its founder, Rudolf Steiner, is no longer here. This is why it has to go through the most dreadful disasters. A strength of soul is needed that can be provided only by this society (out of the Christ impulse). No physical efforts can attain it, nor the genius one may have brought along through at birth. Right now, everything is breaking down, and only it remains. Our "I"-building property is that of humanity itself; the word that is cultivated; the

living knowledge; the Society. Now we should step before Rudolf Steiner's central work, the Christ statue, which stands in the Goetheanum, and ask ourselves, "What am I to do? Everyone knows the way, the truth and the life."[178]

Hearing your words, though we succumb to death
We enter deeply into life.
From the profound obscurities of Earth
We glimpse the stars' bright Resurrection light.

Not judged or judging with a backward sight:
No—pointing forward on the paths divine,
Though physical being be utterly destroyed
The cosmic wheel comes circling round again.

And with us in the chariot of the skies
Go Seraphim and Cherubim and Thrones
Bearing upon their wings the solar eyes
Lent them by God and by the Son of Man.

And through them pictures dawn as the veil parts:
Of future destines not yet realized.
The primal power that touched our hearts
Now lives transformed in our perceiving gaze.

Through our tears of joy we gain a view
Of the eternal realm we spirits share
Upon this journey, finding it anew
When once again your word we hear.[179]

2. *The Relationship of the Anthroposophical Society to the Spiritual World*

Stefano Gasperi

Like my friend Peter Selg, I find that the clock is my greatest enemy, but I console myself with an Afghan proverb aimed at us Westerners: "*You have the watches, but we have the time.*" I am not going to tell you anything especially new—nothing you don't already know, but esotericism is not about doing or experiencing new things all the time; it is about continuously planting the same images, the same content, into the soul. That's why I think it is always wonderful to have the opportunity to bring this content to life again together and to experience it in the present. The topic I was given to talk about came as a bit of a shock at first: the Anthroposophical Society and the spiritual world. Is this something one can speak about without being too abstract? But then some images came to me that inspired me for this contribution.

I will begin with two of those images. One is from the Revelation of St. John, chapter 12, where we are given an image of the woman with the child and Michael's struggle with the dragon. We know that the dragon stands before this woman who is about to give birth, waiting to devour her child. We could say that this image from the Apocalypse mirrors the whole tragedy of the twentieth century. The twentieth century has an apocalyptic signature. It was also the time when Anthroposophy and the Michael School incarnated on Earth through Rudolf Steiner. It is a feminine symbol.

Moreover, until the fifteenth century, Europe was not the same political and geographical structure it is today. Europe was the seat of Christianity. Maps of Europe from that time often show a virgin, a female figure, standing on a map of Europe. This is a true soul imagination; it is inscribed into Europe. The following passage is by the well-known Czech philosopher Jan Patočka: "*The history of Europe up to, let's say, the fifteenth century is largely the history of the attempt to nurture the soul. Europe was born from this motif—a motif of nurturing the soul—and it died because such soul nurturing was forgotten.*"[1]

About a hundred years ago, Europe was engulfed in an all-consuming physical and spiritual conflagration, and with World War I a real abyss opened up. Just before and during that time Rudolf Steiner was active. The activities of Rudolf Steiner and the Anthroposophical Society unfolded in the midst of this demonic, fiery battle. Not only did flames destroy our Goetheanum, but—as Rudolf Steiner sadly concluded—the Anthroposophical Society was also in ruin, a "heap of rubble."

Seven years from now, we will celebrate the centenary of the Christmas Conference (2023). What do these two elements have in common? With World War I and the twenty million lives it claimed, the abyss opened. The old social order—just think of all the empires: the German Reich, the Habsburg Monarchy, the Ottoman Empire—was all in pieces. The European countries fought one another with such violence that a giant global cancer could grow and metastasize across the continent. The Christmas Conference and this tragedy belong together like light and shadow. With this opening of the abyss, the drama of the century began; everywhere was division, conflict, and polarization. An abstract spirituality developed and was floating in the air while, on the other hand, the cultural and natural sciences evolved in a form that left them void of soul and spirit; everywhere was division, separation, polarization. The situation was fittingly referred to as a "loss of the middle."

Then a new seed was planted into the world through Rudolf Steiner—the Christmas Conference. As you all know, the Christmas Conference gave us our identity and our spiritual tasks. Rudolf Steiner often used the strange expression "cosmic turning point of time." How are we to understand this? There are many layers to it, of course. One of the ways I understand it is this: only with the Christmas Conference as a seed will we be able to slowly realize what the Mystery of Golgotha has given to the Earth, what it has created and prepared. A seed was planted then; now—after the end of the Kali Yuga, in the new Michael Age—the event can be grasped and realized fully by individuals, in freedom, through Rudolf Steiner's Spiritual Science.

The spirit begins to take effect, and I would like to remind you of the words Rudolf Steiner said to Ita Wegman (cited by my dear colleague and friend Peter Selg) not long before the Goetheanum fire: "What is lacking among the members of the Anthroposophical Society is the genuine affirmation of the spirit; people lack the courage to realize the spirit."[2] You know how intimately the whole of Anthroposophy is connected with the Christ impulse. Rudolf Steiner said, "*The destiny of Anthroposophy wants to be that of Christianity.*"[3]

What was the impulse of the Mystery of Golgotha? I am speaking from the medical point of view when I describe it as a universal healing process, a remedy for the whole of humanity. Christ is quite rightly also called the Healer, and there is a wonderful sentence by Marcellus Empiricus (of Bordeaux), who put together a compendium of ancient medical preparations in Latin. In *De Medicamentis* he wrote, many centuries ago, "*Summum caelum, ima terra, medium medicamentum*" (The heavens above, the Earth below, and medicine in the middle). The medicine in the middle means that healing takes place in the middle, because the human is a being of the middle. The Latin concepts *remedium*, *medicus*, *meditare*, *meditatio,* and so on derive from this view; they are all associated with this word *middle,* the healing of the human being in the middle.

We can also use the image of the wound, for we are as human beings like open wounds. What does the physician do with a wound? Or what is a wound? Medically speaking, a wound is a place where the continuity of tissue is disrupted; normally whole tissue has been torn apart. If we want a wound to heal, we must bring the two sides together and stitch them up. The healing must come from the patient, but it comes from deep inside. If we look at the Mystery of Golgotha as a universal healing process, we could say: the Christ stitches the human being and God, Heaven, and Earth, together again. If you wish, we can also call it an immense process of integration, because the healing of the middle always means the harmonizing of polarizing processes. If we take this seriously, we could say that the main task of Anthroposophy and of the Anthroposophical Society and its members is to heal human beings and to heal humankind.

At the end of the Christmas Conference Rudolf Steiner said in his farewell address to the members, "*Carry these warm hearts to strong, healing actions in the world.*"[4] These words expressed a hope, an encouragement. This confirms what I have said: It is about the healing of (what Rudolf Steiner initially called) the intellectual original sin. It is about the transformation of the entire culture, of all of civilization, as symbolized in the forces of resurrection. This is our main task.

Rudolf Steiner speaks of pathological developments and their healing: "The life of humanity from the fifth post-Atlantean era onward has been a slow process of becoming ill.... All education and culture must aim to heal. Healing is the first true consequence of the Christ impulse. Christ's first and foremost task in the fifth post-Atlantean age is to be the healer, the savior."[5] When we look at Rudolf Steiner's work with this in mind, we find that he was striving for integration in everything he did. The first half of human evolution, until the Mystery of Golgotha, was marked by separation, division, and atomization, all of which affected society and even the individual human being.

Following the Mystery of Golgotha everything needs to be integrated again through the Christ impulse. You remember the words from the Gospel of Matthew: "Where two or three are gathered in my name, there I am among them."[6] This is the original signature of the Christ impulse—to join everything together again. There are wonderful examples in the life of Rudolf Steiner; wherever we look, everywhere we find this principle of integration, even when he explained to Marie Steiner very early on, "This should be our ideal: to create *forms* that are expressions of the inner life."[7] Or when he brought together consciousness and life, form, and content—as in the two domes of the first Goetheanum. Or in the Society—the karmic streams, Platonists and Aristoteleians, young souls and old souls, esoteric and exoteric, Society and movement. Or when we look at all the areas where Anthroposophy is applied in practice: everywhere we see this effort to unite and integrate. We know how difficult this is. In farming, for instance, horn manure and horn silica; or in curative education, point and circle, and so on. This was clearly Rudolf Steiner's main task.

Integration of course also means bridging the gap between individual and society, an incredible problem that is typical of our time. You know that Rudolf Steiner from the beginning, from the beginning of the twentieth century, always cultivated two elements that belong together: the advancement of individual souls and community-building. These impulses are never separate with Rudolf Steiner, although his efforts in this direction were probably not rightly understood at first, because the members were more interested in their own soul development and less in community-building, but one can see how these two components appear together.

So much as an introduction. Another good image came to me on a visit to the Baptistery in Florence. At the time I was, of course, constantly thinking about what I should say at the Goetheanum on this topic. Suddenly I saw it before me in a picture: the Foundation Stone, the whole Christmas Conference, are depicted masterfully in the Baptistery.

The Baptistery was dedicated to John the Baptist, who said, "He must increase, but I must decrease"—or "Change your mind." Rudolf Steiner put it slightly differently: "Learning to think and feel in a new way is what Anthroposophy requires us to do, not just to think and feel other things."[8] And what is this Baptistery? You stand there and above you, in the dome, you see a giant Christ figure and the nine choirs of the hierarchies around the human being. The Baptistery was the place where people were christened. Friedrich Rittelmeyer once said, "*With the Christmas Conference humanity was newly baptized!*"

This Baptistery is octagonal—which is also interesting. The octagon is an architectural solution for creating a transition from a square ground plan—the presbytery—to a round cupola. There is no other way of solving this problem. Eight sides—the eighth day is that of the Resurrection; it is also the day of God, *dies domini*, the Sunday, the day of the Resurrection. In this Baptistery many people were christened, which means that here began the new Adam, a new conversation between human and God—and through this Christ impulse the heavens and the Earth connect again. The octagon harmoniously links the square with the dome, the Earth with the heavens.

Finally, I was comforted, and I thought, *this is it, our Christmas Conference*. I stand here as a modern human being, and in this conversation from above all the hierarchical beings come down in images, with Christ at the center. Here begins something new, here is a germ, something is newly christened, and here I try to lift myself up as a human being to these higher beings. And suddenly the Foundation Stone was there!

The Foundation Stone, with all the choirs, up to the trinity and all the elemental beings, calls to the soul; and here one is surrounded not only by the heavenly hierarchies, but also by all the elemental beings, for the artists have transformed matter here, through color, mosaics, and stone; the elemental beings are transformed, raised to the spirit through the arts. I perceived an incredible depth, a sense of fulfillment—an image of the Anthroposophical Society at the Christmas Conference, with the human being at the center—on Earth, in conversation with the hierarchies.

From this image we now move on and try to see how it is being realized. A new creed begins here—a new union of human beings and gods. I will read a few extracts from the Christmas Conference. At the beginning of the conference Rudolf Steiner said, "This anthroposophical movement is not a service to the Earth. This anthroposophical movement as a whole and in all its parts is a service to the gods, a service to God."[9] A strange way of putting it now (*a new creed*), when human beings wish to elevate themselves as a community to the spiritual world.

All of this becomes clear when we look at the cult that was first given to the Christian Community and then passed on to the Anthroposophical Society: "*The shared experience of the creed as such evokes a sense of community in the human soul.*"[10] "*The Anthroposophical Society also needs such a force so that a sense of community can arise in it.*"[11] A powerful wake-up call! If we want to see what kind of challenge this is we must take it very seriously. It is not so easy; what has been recognized and understood on Earth is now elevated to the suprasensory spiritual realm. "What you have perceived here in the world of the senses suddenly comes to life when you elevate it to the sphere of ideals. It comes to life when you infuse it in the right way with feeling and will impulses."[12] This is the new creed—an inversion of the will impulse.

I spoke of Europe earlier and of the image of the virgin, but there is another image of Europe, for Europe is the place of Christianity: the image of the cross. The cross—two intersecting bars—stands as a physical symbol in Europe. The situation of Christianity is tragic because this cross no longer exists. We have two open wounds again in Europe today: one was inflicted by the separation of the Eastern Church from Rome, and the other later by the division in the Anglican world. The earlier East–West schism was followed by a later North-South schism. The two bars no longer cross but are separate from each other. Historically, I could mention the famous Council of Trent, which caused another tragic north-south division, between the Protestant and the Catholic world. No cross exists now. Tragically, humanity did not act appropriately when the healing could have begun. It did not take Rudolf Steiner seriously. Even bloodier, open wounds were caused when, during World War II, the north–south division was reinforced by Hitler and Mussolini and the horizontal schism by Churchill and Stalin.

Anthroposophy and the Anthroposophical Society would have the potential to heal these wounds forever. Just think of our Foundation Stone Meditation, which refers to this cross without actually mentioning it when it speaks of the elemental beings: in East, West, North, and South. The motif is clearly there.

But the two bars cross in one point, which brings me to my most important concern; the two bars must cross, and the crossing point is the threshold. The Anthroposophical Society, insofar as I know, is the only esoteric movement that refers with such earnestness to the threshold and the guardian. No other esoteric movement does this: they just leave it out. The questions are: Are we taking this problem seriously enough? How do we feel about the threshold, about the guardian? The threshold is at this crossing point, and there we see something important: It is immediately clear which tasks fall to the various areas of life—education, anthroposophic medicine, the arts, and biodynamics. But what are the tasks of the Anthroposophical Society itself? This is not an obvious question. I believe that many young people today are reluctant to join the Society because the question as to why one should become a member of the Society needs to be answered in an entirely different way from how it was answered in the past. And if we don't answer this question clearly enough, our branches will be nothing more than nice and interesting study groups; there will be no progress. The Anthroposophical Society has its own esotericism, and this is what we need to take seriously. The problem surrounding the threshold and the guardian is most important.

We see the cross with its two bars. And that means we need to realize these two parts if we wish to do justice to the creed. There is a horizontal bar, represented by our Society and the relationship we have with one another. And there is the vertical bar, signifying the relationship we have with the higher hierarchies and the spiritual world. What is the spiritual world? The spiritual world is an infinite sum of spiritual beings, from the elemental beings to the higher hierarchies. But that is not all. The spiritual world also encompasses the unborn souls and the souls of the dead;

and into this spiritual world we go every night. When we see the Anthroposophical Society in relation to the spiritual world, we must imagine this immense community, because it belongs to our Anthroposophical Society. And with all these beings we have to form a real relationship. Two bars, the point in which they cross; here is the threshold: *In Christ death becomes life* (*in Christo morimur*). That is the point we have to get to.

Now we need to look at this more closely and ask ourselves which is the right way of communicating with the beings of the spiritual world, for Rudolf Steiner also pointed out that this can be done in the wrong way, particularly in relation to the third hierarchy.

Fostering a connection with the beings of the spiritual world used to be the task of the ancient mysteries. The mysteries used to cultivate this relationship, and Rudolf Steiner provided very precise information about them, above all in the lecture course on the Apocalypse, which he gave to the Christian Community priests. There he described how humanity used to receive help in ancient times. We find a wonderful passage on this in the priest cycles: "*The essential aspect of the ancient mysteries was that the gods came down from their divine thrones to the human beings, and that human beings communicated directly, from being to being, with these gods, in priestly dignity.*"[13] Spiritual beings conveyed their power and impulses to humanity then, but now, in the age of human freedom, humanity is left to itself. The spiritual forces no longer stream down with the same potency.

Rudolf Steiner said that we receive these forces every night when we dwell in the spiritual world, because there we partake of the cosmic thinking, feeling, and will. In the morning, when we wake up, we feel refreshed by these forces. According to Rudolf Steiner the higher beings acquired these forces through self-knowledge, by resolutely working on themselves, and as a result they are able to bestow them on us as gifts. But this possibility is now coming to an end: "*We know that certain forces in the macrocosm begin to run out, and that we are going toward a future when too little will stream down from these higher worlds if human beings do not strive to develop their own souls; for the forces that can stream down are beginning to run out. This is the time in which we live.*"[14]

This is tragic. What will the consequences be for humanity if people are not sufficiently aware of this and if they do not help the hierarchies? Spiritual Science "foresees that, if too few people can be found in the coming centuries who will work their way up into the spiritual worlds, the human race will be increasingly less able to draw forces from the spiritual worlds. We will end up depleted of spiritual strength and human life will grow evermore desolate. People will be too weak to take on their tasks in the world. Human life will dry out, like a tree that has run out of vital juices."[15] Then we will suddenly see the tasks that lie ahead of us. Future evolution will not be possible without our help. We must reach up to help these beings: there is work to do for each individual member, for the branches, for the societies in the various countries, for the General Anthroposophical Society. We could say that the Anthroposophical Society in all its manifestations should be a permanent field of practice, a laboratory for the human being. It should be the pulsating, breathing center between spiritual and human beings, the School for Spiritual Science and its sections, the individual and the Society. You are familiar with Section 1 of the Bylaws: "The Anthroposophical Society is an association of people whose will it is to nurture the life of the soul, both in the individual and in human society, on the basis of a true knowledge of the spiritual world."[16]

Care of the soul life is the main objective; it is the new transubstantiation. I have spoken of a new creed, and in what we know as the sect of the middle (or culmination), transubstantiation is the preliminary stage to the communion. Matter is transformed. Matter needs to be transformed, or transubstantiated, before we can achieve true communion. What is this *matter,* or mercurial substance, that needs to be transformed and in which all polarities need to be integrated? It is our soul. The soul integrates all polar processes—past and future, sympathy and antipathy, body and spirit. The soul is our main area of practice. It is no coincidence that the Foundation Stone Meditation addresses the soul so pointedly ("Human soul! Practice..."). It indicates that nurturing the soul, the soul life—what is universally human—is our main task.

At the beginning of my talk I cited Jan Patočka: The history of Europe is the history of how the soul was—or was not—nurtured. How do we do this nurturing in practice? Recently, in Vienna, I mentioned how, at a meeting of general secretaries with the Executive Council, Sergei O. Prokofieff asked everyone present what the Anthroposophical Society meant to them. To keep it very brief, my predecessor Stefano Pederiva, who was general secretary of the Anthroposophical Society in Italy for twenty-one years, put it very beautifully. He said, "For me the Anthroposophical Society is the place where people, in a familial way, support, care for, protect and help each other to cross the threshold."

In the mystery dramas we read that, in ancient times, the person to be initiated was always surrounded by twelve hierophants, because of the dangers and problems awaiting. Each of the hierophants had the task of protecting a part of the new initiate.

Today, the question is this: Where are the people who protect us from potential errors, weaknesses, mistakes, and such? I think that is the wonderful secret of being members of a branch. I can honestly say that I have experienced this in forty years of continuous branch work, and that I have learned so much. I always observe (for me this is a signature) that members who isolate themselves and withdraw from the community tend to wander on strange paths. Many become ill, mentally or physically, or their view of Anthroposophy becomes one-sided and dogmatic. This seems to indicate that we expose ourselves to greater dangers if we do not choose the familial way of working together in the community, because mutual esoteric–therapeutic support and protection are missing. I find the thought very interesting that the Society can be the place where people help and support one another so they can cross the threshold in a healthy way. It is a new way of looking at it. One could say that this is where the true esotericism of the Anthroposophical Society begins. Here begin the tasks that I have mentioned earlier—for the individual member, for the branches, the societies in the various countries, and the General Anthroposophical Society.

The question now is how we can come closer to the higher beings? How can we meet them? I don't want to answer this question, but a possible way might be to plant high ideals into our souls. What is an ideal? An ideal is something like a seed, something that lies in the future, but that is real and present in certain beings in the spiritual world. Friedrich Benesch once put this very aptly when he said, "In Michael selflessness is a reality." When we plant the ideals that the hierarchies already have into ourselves, the forces arising from this can bring us closer to these beings. And the esoteric side of the branch life will become more apparent. You know that it was Rudolf Steiner's concern from the very beginning that the anthroposophical work should be done in communities—study groups or, later, branches—because he knew that this was the main task of the mysteries at all times. It was how the next era was prepared.

This was the task of the initiates in the mysteries, but it had to be carried out communally, not by individuals. Moreover, the ideals upon which we build our branch life tell us how to prepare the sixth cultural era—the age of the spirit self. The spirit self has three properties or moral qualities that we are called on to practice inwardly: brotherliness in the social life; freedom of thought; and knowledge of the spirit. But we cannot put these three ideals into practice unless we work on our soul, overcome the beasts, and transform the three soul forces. "When we unite as brothers and sisters in work groups, something hovers over us that is like a child of the forces of the spirit self, and that is nurtured by the beings of the higher hierarchies, so that it can stream down into human souls when it returns in the sixth cultural era."[17] Rudolf Steiner comments on this further: "The thought that we are doing the work we are doing not solely for ourselves but so that it can stream up into spiritual worlds gives special dignity to a branch."[18]

We can ask why we come together in work groups. Rudolf Steiner's answer was this:

> It is not in vain that people come together in our movement to nurture the more intimate part of our spiritual treasure; they earnestly vow to be together in familial love and concord. This is not only important for the way we perceive and deal with each other, or because we can speak with each other entirely differently when we know we speak to kindred souls with whom we are consciously connected. These are not the only reasons. There is something else. What we do when we unite in the individual branches is intimately connected with the view we need to have of our spiritual movement if we understand it truly and profoundly.[19]

"In familial love and concord..." *Concord* (we say *"concordia"* in Italian) is a wonderful word: *cum corde*—with the heart.

These are the basic conditions—familial love and concord, or togetherness. There must be a harmony of sentiments: "By coming together voluntarily, people gather around a center. The feelings that flow together in this center invoke certain beings to work together as a kind of group soul, but in a way very different from the old group souls."[20] Sergei O. Prokofieff studied these aspects profoundly. New social communities form when feelings resonate together here on Earth, in familial love with these new group souls. Yet, everyone who is intensively involved with branch work knows how far and remote we still are from such lofty ideals. I ask myself how much of these high ideals lives in me, how much of this brotherliness, of this love and of the interest in other members? Freedom of thought means active tolerance. And spirit knowledge? This refers to a strict, cognitive effort needed in our branch work so that it does not become idle chat or a place for dogmatism and pedantry, ambition or sophistry. We know our weaknesses. It is little wonder that the Anthroposophical Society with its branches becomes evermore depleted. We notice the loss of the middle here, too.

When the center is lost, the strength of our movement is disseminated into the areas of work and the School for Spiritual Science. But it needs a strong center to keep the two elements in harmony because otherwise the Society will grow thin and age.

In Italy we have gained sixty-two new members this year, none of them younger than thirty-two. And unlike societies in other countries, ours is not even so old. Also: forty of these sixty-two joined as individuals rather than as members of a branch. People do not only have difficulties connecting with the Society, they are also reluctant to connect with a particular branch. They want to be free. This is an expression of something we have ourselves to blame for. Why is our branch life not attractive? Why can't we even manage the work we do on behalf of humanity, the nurturing of the soul, among ourselves? If we do not manage this we will only feed illusions.

I don't mean to be pessimistic; I see what I am saying as an encouragement to do things better. Because I believe that there is hope for the future, and for the Anthroposophical Society, if we strengthen the branch work and improve its quality. These high ideals, or at least the attempt to come closer to them, immediately bring up new questions. How can we motivate people, younger people, to join the Society? How can we change our branch life so that we, amongst ourselves, can at least try to realize these ideals as much as possible? How is it with this universally human endeavor when it comes to the refugee question? People are coming to Europe from an entirely different background, a different consciousness; they come from the realm of the sentient soul, from the third and fourth cultural era, to Europe where the consciousness soul has already become established.

How do we integrate this? Is it not a problem, or task, of the Anthroposophical Society to foster that which is universally human? How can two religious traditions as disparate as Islam and Christianity be integrated? Or in a continent such as Europe, where we have two large monotheistic blocs? Natural science is, in truth, monotheistic. From the other side come the dogmatic religions that are also monotheistic and have no concepts for our culture, no concept of the trinity. How can one find the Christ if one only has one concept of god? How about fundamentalism, which has a god but no human being, whereas in Europe secularization has brought us to a point where we have human beings but no god? God without human beings or human beings without god: the healthy middle has been lost—another difficult challenge. I do not want to give answers, but I see tasks everywhere! A young member in our branch once told me, "I am not interested in a group where each of my questions is immediately answered." The lecturing has to stop, I think, for Anthroposophy will otherwise remain a doctrine. Rudolf Steiner said that we must change from a society of knowledge into a society of actions.

The Anthroposophical Society has its own task in this respect. The branches are places where we can practice, where the other member is my threshold. The threshold is not only above: there is also a horizontal threshold, and that is the other person who mirrors me. There I meet my shadow, my beasts. Rudolf Steiner had a reason for saying, in 1923, that we should practice the six ancillary exercises. They are the instruments for developing heart thinking, the quality of the heart: "Yes, my dear friends, the Anthroposophical Society certainly needs all of the six virtues and it must strive to acquire these virtues."[21] I think branches, anthroposophical communities, would be wonderful places today to practice these six ancillary exercises together. They need work but they are a great help on the way to self-knowledge.

Now I come to my final thought. I have described what I see as the tasks of our branches, as the esoteric aspect of our Anthroposophical Society, but that is, of course, just one of many layers. The relationship of the Anthroposophical Society with the spiritual world is one layer. In some lectures Rudolf Steiner also described the wrong path. How can one relate to the third hierarchy in an unhealthy way? He speaks of omissions and errors, of people not having sufficiently transformed the three soul forces; and he speaks in quite a dramatic way of the consequences such omissions could have for the third hierarchy and how such errors could affect the angels, archangels, and archai. These are the beings with whom we, as members of an esoteric society, seek to establish a connection. Individuals seek to connect with their own angel or with the angel of another person; the task of the societies in the individual countries is with the folk spirit and that of the General Anthroposophical Society is with the spirit of the age. This is the correct way. Problems can also arise if we are asleep when we pass the guardian of the threshold. We have spoken about the new creed; for the branch life the highest form of creed is the formation of karma. According to Rudolf Steiner the branches have the esoteric task of bringing karma into order.

I started to talk about the apocalyptic signature of the century, of how World War I opened up an abyss, and how World War II, as a logical consequence of this, led to further division, fragmentation, and polarization. I have tried to show that the Mystery of Golgotha was a powerful healing process, and how two thousand years later, guided by Rudolf Steiner, we as individuals and as a community take on the task of achieving this healing process for humankind. We have a name for this integrative force: there is only one force that can integrate everything because this force contains everything—nothing needs to stay outside—and that is the power of love.

Love is, as you all know, the result of the harmonious interaction of thinking, feeling, and will—when the soul is well nurtured. And that is the task of our Society once the soul has become virginal again.

> Enveloped by loving thoughts, the light of true humanity shall shine out through Anthroposophy. Knowledge is just the form that makes it possible for human beings to gather in their hearts the true spirit from the wide expanses of the cosmos so that, from there, it can illumine human thoughts. And because Anthroposophy can really only be grasped through love, it engenders love when it is truly understood by human beings.... In Anthroposophy words are not formed in the same way as they are formed elsewhere in our time. Words are really pleas. Each word in Anthroposophy, if spoken in the right way, is a plea, a prayer: that the spirit may descend to human beings.[22]

I think this plea is directed toward us as a challenge, or appeal, with which we can joyfully, enthusiastically, and confidently stride toward the future despite all the difficulties in the world.

I shall finish as I have started. At the beginning I described the Baptistery in Florence. Our great poet, Dante, lived in Florence. Dante is, as far as I know, one of the few authors who described the three beasts before Steiner did. His great opus, *The Divine Comedy*, is the poetic counterpart of the Baptistery in Florence. The *Divine Comedy* describes the journey of the human being toward self-knowledge, overcoming the beasts in three steps, until the human being returns through the choirs of the hierarchies up to the trinity. And you know that the *Divine Comedy* ends in paradise with the famous words, "*L'amor che move il sol e l'altre stelle*" (It is love that moves the Sun and the other stars).

Grazie!

Mario Betti (right) with Heinz Georg Häussler in 1967
(*Betti,* Leben im Geiste der Anthroposophie. Eine Autobiografie, *Arlesheim 2015*)

3. My Existential Relationship with the Anthroposophical Society

Mario Betti

I have been a member of the General Anthroposophical Society for fifty years and am pleased to be able to talk to you, as members of the Swiss Society, about my relationship with the Society and the School for Spiritual Science, because it was in Switzerland that this relationship began.

I was asked to approach the topic from a biographical point of view and will therefore very briefly describe the three essential steps I took in this relationship.

I was born in Italy in 1942 and grew up there. I first met Anthroposophy in Rome in 1964 during my military service.

When I became a member in 1965, I lived in Zurich, and the first branch meetings I attended took place there in Lavaterstrasse. I think back with gratitude to personalities such as Mr. Mohr-Bleuler, Dr. Peter Mensching and his wife, and Dr. Laubi, who received me so hospitably when I was only twenty-three. At the time I was working in the administration of the Dolder Grand Hotel in Zurich, and a year later I moved to Dornach, having decided to reorient myself professionally. During the following year, 1967, I joined the School for Spiritual Science.

I experienced the beginning of my membership as a particularly positive time. The Christmas Conference of 1923 and all that was connected with it filled me with enthusiasm.

Everything was simply wonderful in the Dornach Empire! I felt like Abel, who lived his shepherd life in the green pastures of the Lord. I worked as a security officer at the Goetheanum and absorbed Anthroposophy like a dry sponge! At the time there were many people in Dornach who had still experienced Rudolf Steiner personally. Working under the same roof with personalities such as Friedrich Hiebel, Karl von Baltz, Rudolf Grosse, Herbert Witzenmann, and others, was simply amazing.

Over time, doubts kept creeping in as to the authenticity of this Elysium. I heard about past conflicts, exclusions, and other divisions. In February 1968 the so-called book crisis unfolded. I experienced awful—sometimes smaller, sometimes larger—membership meetings where people had no-holds-barred fights with one another. Another split threatened to shake the Society.

In the fall of 1968 I followed a call from Italy and moved to Verona in order to work there for Anthroposophy, the Waldorf School movement, and the goals of the Christmas Conference. Extraneous circumstances then led me to Germany in the late fall of 1971, where I still live today. I became a Waldorf teacher and later a lecturer at Alanus University in Alfter near Bonn and at the Stuttgart Waldorf Teacher Training Institute.

While still in Verona I became quite active as a lecturer and author. My profound relationship with the Society and the School for Spiritual Science gradually developed some cracks over the years, however; I grew increasingly unhappy with the way the Society developed and was run from Dornach. This was, of course, *my point of view*, because other people felt that a fresh wind was bringing new life to the Dornach pastures.

I felt more and more that what was happening in Dornach was not suited to bringing the different—the Platonic and the Aristotelian—streams together. Rudolf Steiner had spoken repeatedly of how important it was for the future of our civilization that these two streams come together. This working together has always been a central aspect of my work in the Society and in the School for Spiritual Science.

A *Cainite* indignation grew within me and, in 1995, I stopped being a class member (for three years) and also considered withdrawing from the Anthroposophical Society. *Abel* had disappeared from my soul. Those were very painful years for me.

I was led to apply again for membership in the School for Spiritual Science and to give up my plan of leaving the Society as the result of a particular realization—Rudolf Steiner has to bear the karmic consequences of his actions like anyone else, especially following the new foundation of the Society and the School for Spiritual Science.

I became a class member again, mostly in order to help him to bear the immense burden of the foundation of the Society and of the School for Spiritual Science. This was the internal aspect of this process. The essential external turning point was—after some altercations between Dornach and myself—a long conversation I had with Heinz Zimmermann in Alfter. As a member of the Executive Council he told me, "The Executive Council had neglected to enter into dialogue with me on this matter." If I wished, I could be regarded as a member of the School for Spiritual Science again, and this happened soon afterward without any official formalities. What had made the difference for him was my relationship with the Christmas Conference.

How has this relationship with the Society continued to develop? Over the years I had increasingly experienced that the society, *as it had become*, was dead. But as I continued to deepen the Foundation Stone meditatively, I realized that this "foundation stone of love" was an active reality that sought to have a *direct* impact on the social life. The substance of this "foundation stone of love," which is forged from wisdom and love, seemed to me to be a part of Rudolf Steiner's own being. This substance alone, I felt, could give the global Anthroposophical Society the spiritual impetus it needs to continue its mission of spiritualizing all of civilization. In meditative deepening, or in dialog with Rudolf Steiner's being, this meditation ignited a kind of Grail flame in the heart region, like the objective result of an alchemical process—a flame as an intense inspiration and devotion to the goals of the Society and the School for Spiritual Science.

This foundation stone needs less scholarly interpretation, even though this is also very important. It needs to become effective in direct human encounters—here and now. This is what I continue to see as the precondition for an enhanced effectiveness of our Michael community in today's world.

Thanks to this Grail flame, thanks to the small resurrection that occurred within me, I found both Cain and Abel in my soul again, but now reconciled and reunited.

They are now pleased to work together for "*Anthroposophia*," for the cultural mission of Spiritual Science.

First Question and Answer Session

"Thank you so much for sharing your experiences with us. How do you think we can achieve the goals you mentioned? What do we need to consider?"

I start with the two main substances that comprise the "dodecahedral stone of love": wisdom and love. The tragedy that has been haunting the Anthroposophical Society for decades is not that we are lacking in knowledge or wisdom. What has been missing, even from the great original Council, was not wisdom but love. Those truly great personalities had not learned to love each other and to deal with each other accordingly—with disastrous consequences.

I don't mean this in any sentimental way. The love I speak of is the immediate love that is experienced in human encounters as a threshold where *light and warmth* alone make all boundaries disappear—particularly the karmic boundaries that often make us seem like shadow beings to each other. I speak of the love described by Paul in his first letter to the Corinthians, of love as the universal power that made the Resurrection possible on the very first Easter Sunday. It is the same universal power that inspired Rudolf Steiner continuously—the love of which he said in *Esoteric Science* "arises from the wisdom reborn in the 'I'"—the whole purpose of Earth evolution. Wisdom is reborn in the "I," not in the head. No spirit-children are born from the head but only brain-children, and they speak the language of death. Rudolf Steiner was a living example of this wisdom and love. And his example lights the way for us like a distant star. And I am sure that if we manage to keep the Grail flame alive, of which I spoke earlier, our Society can grow only stronger, and our contemporaries will not walk past us. The work in our institutions will also grow more fertile.

I think of an anecdote that has been with me for many decades: Two priests complained to Gandhi that the Hindus were refusing to accept the message of the Sermon on the Mount—a fact they found incomprehensible. Gandhi told them, "Do as the rose does. Everyone loves it because it gives of its pleasant fragrance. Do just that, gentlemen!" Please excuse my being so open, but when I am asked so directly I can only answer truthfully.

SECOND QUESTION AND ANSWER SESSION

"You spoke of the difficulties Platonic souls have in our Society and of the necessity for both streams—the Platonic and the Aristotelian—to work together. What should be done, in your view, so that this collaboration happens, and what could be improved so that the Platonists connect better with the Society and the School for Spiritual Science?"

I have struggled with this riddle for many decades and have attempted a first answer in my book about Platonism and Aristotelianism, which came out in 2003. I even had the opportunity to give two lectures on the topic in this auditorium in 2003. This was during a conference that marked the 800th anniversary of the death of Alanus ab Insulis (Alain de Lille). Frank Teichmann had just given two wide-ranging lectures on the Cathedral and School of Chartres, and I tried to pursue this thread to the present time and into the future by speaking of a new Platonism.

To summarize briefly, I see the historical development of the two streams as three steps that complemented each other: first there was the original Platonism and Aristotelianism in ancient Athens and its global dissemination in the following centuries. *Then*, with the internalization of the heart forces initiated by Christianity, also in relation to knowledge, we see the flourishing of the School of Chartres in the Middle Ages as the center of Platonic spirituality and the emergence of the Dominican Order. The latter was really the continuation and promotion of a refinement of thinking, to the degree that was possible in the age of the rational soul. And *finally*, as we reach the nineteenth and twentieth century, we first observe the immense—primarily Aristotelian—step Rudolf Steiner took toward the spiritualization of intelligence.

On the basis of the *Philosophy of Freedom* and other works—for the crystal mountain of spiritualized Aristotelianism must not be circumnavigated—a third phase of Platonism is now possible, Platonism that aims to work, when it comes to knowledge, in the light and power of Christ's reappearance and has an immediate impact on the social life. I will mention *just one* aspect of its all-embracing effectiveness, especially since the idea of beauty seems to be intrinsic to Platonism. People in antiquity turned to the *transcendent idea* of beauty. The task today is to transform what is *earthly into ideas* through the power of the Resurrected. Because the Resurrected is not only true and good but also of solar beauty—beauty that anticipates the brilliance of a new, transformed light-Earth, beauty that can light up, especially, in the encounter mentioned earlier.

This encounter may at first be an expression of old, negative karma. But through the resurrected Christ, who can transform anything into solar beauty, something new can be born. Yes: what is old and dead can be transformed into light-Earth. Through him we can also explore the beauty of the other and immediately create social substance. Then we can say to our sister or brother, "Let me discover your beauty" or "Tell me about yourself so I can see you better." Then we will build bridges to others. This human-social approach applies to all streams, of course, because Platonism, like Aristotelianism, is not a private matter of a group of "chosen people," but a global impulse of our time—just like other global impulses are important at other times.

Now, Platonists are often somewhat unconventional or individual and not easy to understand for Aristotelians. It can be the other way round, too, of course, but I think that in our movement *Plato is the one who is misunderstood*, as Rudolf Steiner once said in a particular historical context.[1]

I give you one example: At the big world conference for members of the School for Spiritual Science in 1993, here, in the almost full main auditorium, the general secretary of a society in a European country spoke about his country's plans to further develop the Society and the School for Spiritual Science. He said, among other things, something like, "Well, all these plans were somewhat 'Platonic,'" and as he said this he made an upward spiral movement with this right hand in order to show that the Platonic is not grounded and therefore airy. I was outraged because it was such a serious situation, seven years before the millennium. I asked to speak several times so I could correct this but did not get through—not even in the afternoon because, mysteriously, the list for spontaneous contributions was already full.

I had often heard the view expressed that Platonists are essentially "feeling" types and therefore unable to *form* their thinking. But what about the great thinkers of Chartres: Gilbert de la Porrée, Bernardus Silvestris, John of Salisbury, Alain de Lille, and so on. And Rudolf Steiner speaks of the necessary *further* spiritualization of Aristotelianism as a Spiritual Science through the Platonists. How about Aristotelians developing a greater understanding for their brothers and sisters, as a foundation for working together on equal terms? Platonists do not proceed from the form to the content. They start from the content and try to give it form. Let us look, from a sociological point of view as it were, at Raphael's School of Athens: Aristotle's gesture goes downward—a *formative* gesture. There is a danger of formalism here.

Plato points upward and this can today, in the sense of the resurrected, only mean *transformation*. Platonists start from the *content* of their soul and seek to give it form, a form that can also subsist from the point of view of Christian beauty. The danger here is a lack of form.

In principle, the Christmas Conference Society offers a home to both orientations. Rudolf Steiner formed it from above—there was no alternative at the time. Is this form still valid today, almost a hundred years later? Should we not develop a new form that resonates with the "old souls"—maybe also for the School for Spiritual Science—so that more people can find a home here, whether or not they are Platonists?

What I find attractive in the Swiss Society is that it is being built from the bottom up, *from a spiritual basis*, and not from the top down, based on a sense of entitlement derived from tradition and bylaws. It is not that decisions cannot succeed in this way, but—in my view anyway—an approach suited to Platonists needs to start from the "basis;" it must be founded on a mutually recognized spiritual competence, in esoteric questions, too—and, of course, in concord with the "leadership," but that means in a familial way.

To summarize: the further development of the Anthroposophical Society based on the cooperation of the two streams depends, in my view, more than ever on the silent factor I referred to earlier as *factual* wisdom and love. I mean the "foundation stone of love" that is valid for all of humanity.

4. *The Universal Temple*

Johannes Greiner

"And only when our brothers' aims
unite for peaceful purposes
with those the heretics pursue,
can good in earthly progress blossom forth."

RUDOLF STEINER[1]

"One can do but little alone, but he can avail who in the proper hour unites his strength with others," says the old man with the lamp in Goethe's fairytale, *The Green Snake and the Beautiful Lily.*[2] The Anthroposophical Society was founded so that many could "unite in the proper hour" and work against cultural decay, planting a new spiritual impulse in a humanity that had become pervaded by materialism. This Society is for all those who feel the deep inner need for such a new spirituality. The more varied the colors that unite in this society the more interesting and fruitful it will be. Goethe's fairytale gives us an indication of how important it is that a great diversity of people from all spiritual backgrounds comes together in the temple. This thought was further developed in the four mystery dramas, which Rudolf Steiner composed and arranged to be performed in Munich. These dramas illustrate the chances and the drama involved in the meeting and working together of a group of very different individuals. The second and fourth mystery dramas in particular show painfully what happens when people who should work together toward the advancement of the spiritual life on Earth are unable or unwilling to do this. We also meet the spiritual powers that prevent such unity: Lucifer and Ahriman, the spirits of the polar positions between which each of us needs to find the golden middle.

The Anthroposophical Society could be a temple for the most diverse people from the most diverse karmic backgrounds. Only when everyone who wishes to be part of this Society can be part of it, and only when each one has assumed their rightful place in the temple, will it be possible to achieve for humanity what can be achieved only when people unite and work together toward a higher goal.[3]

This brings up questions: Do they each have a place? Is everyone in the right place? Do we perceive each other sufficiently to be aware of the unity? What do we do when people quarrel? How do we deal generally with opposing positions? How do we find peaceful and yet inspiring ways of working together? The way modeled by Rudolf Steiner at the Christmas Conference of 1923/1924 strikes me as a good example.

The Christmas Conference is a social legacy for us. Rudolf Steiner appointed five very different individuals to the Executive Council. You couldn't have found a group of individuals more dissimilar than Marie Steiner, Ita Wegman, Elisabeth Vreede, Albert Steffen, and Guenther Wachsmuth, who belonged to different karmic streams. Rudolf Steiner brought them together hoping they would be able to work together as representatives of these streams.

Marie Steiner wrote of the Anthroposophical Society's Executive Council, which was instituted at the Christmas Conference: "*The most profound esotericism could ensue from bringing about a harmonious balance between the formerly divergent spiritual streams in some of its representatives. This esoteric task could have been achieved with the help of Dr. Steiner, with his superior insight, strength and capacity for love.*"[4]

Had this been successful, these individuals would have planted a seed for peace that could have grown and benefited all those who are karmically connected with them. The bridge Marie Steiner and Ita Wegman could have built between themselves could have been a positive influence on those standing behind either of them. What this small group could have developed would have been of benefit to humanity as a whole.

The situation was very different with the Executive Council of the first Society, founded in 1913. It consisted of three individuals who were very close: Marie Steiner, Carl Unger, and Michael Bauer. The principle then seemed to be that people should work together who were able to do this well and efficiently.

This was not the case with the Executive Council of the Christmas Conference of 1923. The five individuals thrown together then could not have been more different. Additionally, there was the growing problem arising from Rudolf Steiner's increasingly intimate cooperation and close relationship with Ita Wegman that was difficult to bear for his wife, Marie Steiner.

What united the members of that Executive Council was their individual connection with Rudolf Steiner, which differed, however, in terms of intensity, depth, and how far they went back. There was great potential for conflict in such an inhomogeneous group, and this potential could be overcome only through great effort and peacefulness. Why make things so difficult? Why did Rudolf Steiner not appoint another group that shared the same karmic background?

The only possible explanation is that he considered it important that the different karmic streams would find a way of working together. This is why he gave the almost eighty lectures on karma following the Christmas Conference, as well as the Christmas Conference lecture course, *World History in the Light of Anthroposophy*, which can be seen as the foundation for the karma lectures.

Why did the different streams have to coalesce? Anthroposophy is closely connected with Michael, the spirit of time and archangel of the Sun. Michael is interested in human beings as "I"-beings and as members of humanity as a whole. Attributes such as race, ethnicity, language, gender, karmic streams are irrelevant to him. Michaelic wisdom can never belong to one particular group, such as Dominicans, Franciscans, or Platonists. Any group can only find access to Michael's wisdom if they are willing to connect with humanity as a universal entity. The more we are part of humanity, the closer we come to Anthroposophy. The more we pursue the separate interests of a particular karmic stream, the more we separate ourselves from Michael and his influence.

Rudolf Steiner developed Anthroposophy with all kinds of people. It is amazing how different the people were that he worked with. They could all relate to him. The diversity of Anthroposophy is owed to the fact that people from all karmic backgrounds came to Rudolf Steiner with their questions. He brought Anthroposophy as something that concerned humankind as a whole, as an answer to the questions and needs of the most diverse individuals.

Because such an inclusive gift to humanity cannot be maintained and nurtured by people of one stream, the Executive Council of the Christmas Conference had to include representatives of the most diverse streams connected with Anthroposophy. The institution of the "original council" at the Christmas Conference can therefore be seen as the attempt to keep Anthroposophy for humanity rather than have it monopolized by one particular karmic stream. In this context, Heinz Eckhoff wrote:

> When Rudolf Steiner appointed five personalities to the Esoteric Council at the Christmas Conference of 1923, he knew that behind each of these representatives of the most diverse spiritual streams stood members who had a particular relationship of trust with one of them. The karmic differences of these streams could have been bridged if the impulse of the Christmas Conference had lived strongly enough in the souls to overcome personal interests in favor of supra-personal—Christian—ones. Putting "karma in order" was a fundamental motif of the Christmas Conference, in keeping with the new direction introduced by the Christmas Conference: only now the Anthroposophical Society is shown the "great mirror," in which it can see itself reflected, and in which individual members can see their reflection as well as the karma that has led them to the Anthroposophical Society.[5]

We know that the attempt to create peace failed. Conflicts arose and stifled the group's progress. First Elisabeth Vreede and Ita Wegman were thrown out, then Marie Steiner was ostracized. This meant that not only three karmic streams were suppressed but also the female element as such and the female path to spirituality. Steffen and Wachsmuth remained—the two men who had arguably the least intimate connection with Rudolf Steiner.

This continued: Whenever anyone tried to warn those in charge, they were branded "enemies of the Goetheanum" or "opponents of the anthroposophical cause" and pushed aside. The possibility for corrective self-knowledge was eliminated. There is no doubt, however, that there were also real enemies of Anthroposophy.

It is shocking to see the parallels between the external historical development and that of the Executive Council of the Anthroposophical Society between 1933 and 1945. One can compare the situation with a nuclear fission on various levels. National Socialism brushed aside Europe's culture of the "I." In America, and then Japan, the core of matter was destroyed by the invention and use of the nuclear bomb, and in Dornach the Executive Council broke apart when Vreede and Wegman were excluded.

It is usually futile to speculate about what "might have happened if..." Yet, we can ask ourselves in all earnestness, what would have happened if, while hell broke loose in the world with Hitler and nuclear research, there had been enough peaceful forces in Dornach to continue the communal work inaugurated by Rudolf Steiner? What could have been prevented?

Of course, the people around the Council members would have had to be more helpful, too. Instead, they each held on to the representative of their own stream while rejecting the others. The utter one-sidedness around the individuals in charge exacerbated the fateful polarization.[6]

Have we learned from this? Are we more awake to such developments today? What could we achieve today, if we managed—at a time dominated by the polarizing forces of destructive dogmatic beliefs ("Islamic State") and the unscrupulous materialistic exploitation of people and of the Earth (Western capitalism)—to build bridges of peace between the tendencies in our Society that reflect this outer polarization?

I think that what I have said shows that it is the most urgent task of those who are active within the anthroposophical movement to work together across the boundaries of the different streams, so that out of that diversity a universally human foundation can grow that can carry and support Anthroposophy. The conflicts and fights carried out in the world between the various streams can be settled and peace be made if we focus on the common goals of Anthroposophy. This internal peace can then radiate out into the wider world.

A small group is expected to achieve what is one day to be achieved by all. If this group is successful its success can seep through—homeopathically as it were—to humanity as a whole. The war of all against all can then be overcome, and a community can grow in which the spirit of humanity, which we can also call the Christ, can live as a spirit of peace.

There are beings that strive to prevent this. They go about their work by sowing seeds of discord among the members of groups who then meet in opposition, and the strife among them renders impossible any middle way.

I have an inner image of dark wolves creeping about human communities, sniffing them out. Where they smell disagreement they try to drag it into the light and increase it. Those who give in to them soon get stuck in their contrasting positions, defending them evermore relentlessly.

Eventually they lose their own center. All communal efforts are destroyed, and those who decided before their birth to work together in peace are prevented from realizing those plans because the social terrain has become furrowed with terrible trenches caused by their disagreements.

Ahriman, the spirit of intellectual coldness and materialism, follows the principle of "divide and rule!" Where human communities crumble under the weight of their conflicts, Anthroposophy is no longer a threat to him. He fears nothing more than human communities united under the sign of spiritual thinking, feeling, and doing.

The powers that seek to prevent the healthy middle brought about National Socialism, the atomic bomb, and the break-up of the General Anthroposophical Society in the middle of the twentieth century.

Often the middle path between two extremes is the healthy option. Anthroposophy therefore thrives best in the middle between Aristotelianism and Platonism. But there are other centers, too. When polarization occurs, the middle is no longer possible. The good in the world no longer has any ground to stand on. No one can lay claim to the good. It must be able to live among us.

In 1919, Rudolf Steiner said in Zurich:

> Since the Mystery of Golgotha occurred in Earth evolution, everything relating to human coexistence belongs, in a way, to this Christ impulse. This is most essential: that the Christ impulse does not belong to individuals but to human coexistence. It is, according to Christ Jesus himself, a great error to believe that individuals can have a direct relationship with the Christ. What is important to keep in mind is that Christ lived, died, and rose from the dead for humanity as a whole.[7]

Two people with different views who work together peacefully form the two posts of a doorway through which Christ can enter humanity. If they argue and insist on their individual positions, the two posts move closer together and crash, closing off the middle. There is no way in. The door is closed. There is no opening because the space between the two extremes is gone.

Once I have understood this, I must rejoice about each person who is different from me. The farther away from me this person is, the wider and taller the entrance will be. One must not ask too much of oneself, however. Often it needs many small steps to form or reestablish a center between oneself and another person. Trying to understand the other will help. In the end it is always love and the interest arising from it that will connect people.

We must learn to understand the other's thinking. We should aim for a culture of dialog that can accommodate controversial views without judging and without the expectation that a point can be reached where one view will prevail. Anthroposophy is the consensus within the Anthroposophical Society. Differences can stimulate our thriving to gain self-knowledge, to create peace, and to complement each other. In Albert Steffen's drama *The Fall of the Antichrist,* the artist says to the scientist and to the priest, "Think of the goal you share. Our community has the task of overcoming opposites."[8]

Rudolf Steiner's mystery dramas present examples of the problems confronting those who strive for the spirit or who strive to join other such seekers. He includes the concept of earlier incarnations, showing them also on stage. The actions in former incarnations that have led to particular karmic situations in the present life become clear from these plays.

Central to the second mystery drama, *The Trial of the Soul*, is a look back to an earlier life in medieval times, when many of the individuals living "now" were enmeshed in a difficult conflict. An order of chivalry was already developing the beginnings of modern science, its members anticipating the tasks of the future. They were in conflict with the church because the church desired their possessions and condemned as heresy what the knights considered to be their most sacred mission. The ideological divisions created then and a greed for power have painful consequences in the present life. The monk who "then" tied the son of a knight to himself, separating him from his father, has to learn in his present incarnation as Maria to let go of the pupil who used to be unconditionally devoted to her, and to stop exerting any influence on his soul. The greatest suffering and "soul's trial" ensue for the former pupil, who has now incarnated as the painter Johannes Thomasius. He loves Maria and is reluctant to take even a single step on his spiritual path without her. The coercion in the former life requires a painful process of detachment now.

The knight who, in the Middle Ages, was the father of the young man devoted to the monk and his ecclesiastical teachings, seeks to learn as much as possible from Johannes Thomasius in this life. His aim is to compensate for having deserted his sister in the former incarnation in order to consecrate his life to the goals of the knights. We learn how strong an effect any social wrongdoing has that was committed in an earlier life. What causes the most fateful difficulties "today" are, however, the divisions that occurred in the Middle Ages due to conflicting ideologies. They cause fractures now that can only gradually be balanced and healed.

The story of Simon, the Jew, is most heartrending: he lived a life of loneliness in the Middle Ages because of his belief. The only protection he knows is that of the lords of the castle who think highly of him. He returns in this life as Dr. Strader, who is also alone in the world and only gradually finds access to the community at the center of the mystery dramas.

The drama of the *ancient* tragedy (Aeschylus, Sophocles) is due mostly to the fact that the gods interfere in human lives but are misunderstood by human beings. *Modern* drama is based on the fact that people do not understand one another. Being unable to work with others, although one knows one has a connection with them, or being misunderstood in one's basic intentions—these are the tragedies of life today. We speak of different karmic streams that ought to find peace and connect with one another.

In his mystery dramas, Rudolf Steiner has shown the suffering arising from our failures in this social realm. The second and fourth dramas in particular focus on the inability to work together of people who have to find common ground. In his mystery dramas, Steiner chose images intended to inspire self-knowledge. We are admonished to find out about old habits that are ingrained in us. In former lives, many of us were on the side of the church that branded other streams as heretical. If we do not rid ourselves of old habits, we will continue to carry out an attenuated form of inquisition in the Anthroposophical Society, leading to divisions and painful conflicts. The power we have together will be shattered, and Ahriman will greatly enjoy this. The second mystery drama offers a particularly compelling image of the terrible effect of such belief-based divisions.

In scene 6 of the second drama, young Thomas (Johannes Thomasius in a later life) tells his revered teacher, the monk (later Maria, his lover and spiritual guide), how he found his father again, whom he had lost a long time ago, but how he had now lost him again for good, because his views were opposed to those of the beloved monk:

> I could have quite forgotten all the sorrow
> that he inflicted on my mother and myself,
> as now at last I stood before my father
> who, bowed by sorrow, spoke of bygone days.
> But in him, *your* opponent stood before me.
> One thing alone was clear to me,
> the deep cleft that must sever me forever
> from him I wished so much to love,
> whom ardently so long I sought.[9]

It is shocking to see how different ideologies can be the cause of such division. To his sister, who is trying to establish peace, Thomas explains:

> It is concealed from you, dear sister,
> how power of thought can prove compelling
> once it has gripped the human soul.
> The son does not oppose the father here;
> thought turns away from thought.[10]

Different ways of thinking tear human communities apart. Ideas that are not recognized as being inhumane cause the bondage of individual minds, which in turn results in social rifts. The young man's sister tries to overcome this division with love. What causes strife in the minds of the men (Thomas–the monk–the father) is united in her heart. It is in her that the future is being prepared. In a later life this sister will, as Theodora, announce the etheric appearance of the Christ.[11]

When the monk has to wait in the castle of the despised knights, to whom Thomas' father belongs, the deceased leader of the order appears to him, the saint Benedictus, as well as the tempters Ahriman and Lucifer. The latter embolden him in his condemnation of the knights as heretics and encourage him to investigate their errors in depth. Ahriman in particular, keen to exacerbate the division of the human community, urges the monk to discover the errors of the heretics by praising his attitude:

> You have succeeded well
> in fathoming these brothers' sins
> which they must hide from all the world.[12]

Benedictus, on the other hand, admonishes him to keep his thinking alive. From a wider vantage point, he has now reached into the spiritual world, where the knights' thinking and actions look quite different:

> You find yourself within that Order's house
> which you accuse of evil heresy.
> It seems to hate all that we love
> and to revere what we deem sin.
> Our brothers hold themselves obliged to hasten
> the downfall of this sin against the spirit.
> In this they are supported
> by words which formerly I spoke on Earth.
> They do not dream
> these very words can be renewed only
> if they are nurtured for their further growth
> by those who are successors in my work.

So let arise within your soul
what I once thought in former days on Earth,
but now what it must be
in view of a new age.
. . . .
And only when our brothers' aims
unite for peaceful purposes
with those the heretics pursue,
can good in earthly progress blossom forth.[13]

When he united representatives of different karmic streams on the original Executive Council of the Christmas Conference, Rudolf Steiner pursued such a "peaceful purpose." The same can be attempted again and again. We might improve with constant practice and become better at realizing Rudolf Steiner's legacy and at making an important contribution to world peace.

In the end, all the struggles we have with others are a result of our not being at peace with ourselves. Not striving for inner peace will lead to external conflicts. War within us will lead to war outside of us. This is why the exercises Rudolf Steiner proposed in his book *How to Know Higher Worlds,* or similar exercises from other spiritual streams, are so important. The efforts we undertake in the attempt to advance our inner development can make the world a more peaceful place. In his wonderful autobiography, *Leben im Geiste der Anthroposophie* [life in the spirit of Anthroposophy], Mario Betti writes, "*All recent fundamentalist tendencies are, in my view, rooted in a weakness of the 'I.' Higher development is really an evolutionary mission. Nothing else can bring our civilization forward in all areas.*"[14]

In scene 8 of the second mystery drama, the grand master of the Knightly Order explains the connection between unresolved inner struggles and outer conflicts:

> Those who through the grace of lofty spirit powers
> can turn their gaze upon the souls of human beings
> will see that there the adversaries
> oppose the souls' true being.
> The war our enemies prepare for us
> is but a picture of that mighty battle
> which ceaselessly one power in the heart
> must wage in enmity against the other.[15]

The future of the Society therefore depends on our individual hearts. Whether or not there will be wars depends on each single heart. The crucial decisions are taken in our hearts. There lies the key to community. And there it will be decided whether the temple can become a universal temple: a temple that can embrace all of humanity.[16]

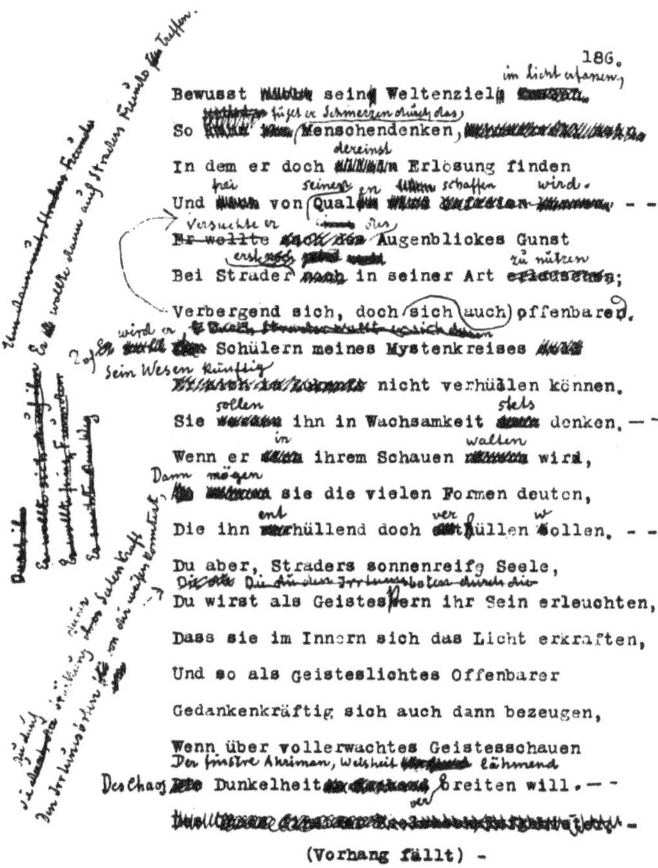

186.

Bewusst sein Weltenziel im Licht erfahren,
So fügt er Schmerzen durch das Menschendenken,
In dem er doch dereinst Erlösung finden
Und frei von Qual seines Schaffen wird. – –
Versuchte er des Augenblickes Gunst
Bei Strader erst in seiner Art zu nützen;
Verbergend sich, doch sich auch offenbarend.
Schülern meines Mystenkreises
Sein Wesen künftig nicht verhüllen können.
Sie sollen ihn in Wachsamkeit stets denken, – –
Wenn er in ihrem Schauen walten wird,
Dann mögen sie die vielen Formen deuten,
Die ihn enthüllend doch verhüllen wollen. – –
Du aber, Straders sonnenreife Seele,
Du wirst als Geistesstern ihr Sein erleuchten,
Dass sie im Innern sich das Licht erkraften,
Und so als Geisteslichtes Offenbarer
Gedankenkräftig sich auch dann bezeugen,
Wenn über vollerwachtes Geistesschauen
Der finstre Ahriman, Weisheit lähmend
Des Chaos Dunkelheit verbreiten will. – –

(Vorhang fällt) –

Rudolf Steiner, hand-corrected typescript: last scene of the fourth mystery drama (CW 44)

5. "Cosmic Midnight Hour"

The Significance of the Mystery Dramas for the Anthroposophical Society

Gioia Falk

The way our Society lives in me today makes me feel I would like to start by saying "*Dear friends of the Society*!" Society cannot be separated from human beings; it is continuously changing, and yet it has an archetype. Rudolf Steiner's mystery dramas reveal how, through inner development, each protagonist's journey not only leads them to self-realization, but also makes their effectiveness on and through each other clear and transparent. The close web of relationships becomes transparent, to the point that we realize how certain actions on a journey are only possible in connection with other people. This transparency can enhance development.

The mystery dramas are like a concentrate of Rudolf Steiner's work—not in a universal but in a concrete, artistic form, individualized as theater. Theater is human destiny: we see individuals on their journey. A person is occupied with him- or herself or with others; in antiquity human destiny was also shared with the gods and spirits. We experience something of this in these dramas, too (Rudolf Steiner called them "our mysteries").

The language used in the mystery dramas invites me to relate the events to myself, even if they are remote from my everyday experience. I enter into dialog with myself. As the events unfold the dimensions widen. We must not see this as an escape from today's reality, but as a necessary pause to understand how events evolve. Rudolf Steiner widens the context of human life to an extent that allows us—for the first time in literature—to experience the immense thought of reincarnation in concrete situations on stage. We see the evolution and transformation of the individual protagonists not through one but many incarnations; we experience the eternal individuality of each in changing manifestations.

And Rudolf Steiner does not stop there. He unfolds an even wider perspective before us by demonstrating that our consciousness does not die after death; halfway through the time between two lives, in the "cosmic midnight hour," we look back on former lives and develop a yearning for a new incarnation. At that point we are, however, not separate individuals as we are in our day-consciousness. We have grown bigger and participate in the process that makes wisdom-filled designs possible, and we experience how other souls, with whom we used to be connected in life, are involved in shaping our destiny, down into the physical body. There is nothing like this anywhere else in literature.

Between 1910 and 1913 such a dimension was presented for the very first time on stage and before an audience. It was the beginning of the industrial age; human beings saw themselves increasingly as godless specks of dust. Rudolf Steiner counterpoised this with his comprehensive spiritual research, which assumed various forms. Now, a hundred years later, the mystery dramas have been performed widely, not only in the German-speaking world, but also in other languages and on other continents.

The mystery dramas have always proved to be inspiring for viewers and readers. In recent years the question that was asked among us repeatedly was what this wider context means for our communities. What does it mean for a future Society? These dramas can provide a new way of understanding life: we notice increasingly that we have more than just the course of a day; we have the night as well, of which we don't know anything initially, but where many daytime experiences are put in order and where skills prepared during the day develop. Today this knowledge tries increasingly to seep through to us. The questions I had in this respect have remained unanswered so far. Maybe there were pressing problems, a feeling of powerlessness, and now the unbearable search for the meaning of life or the causes of my dwindling forces. Can I find some light here? Our time is often described as apocalyptic. The apocalyptic description of the future is coming closer, like a premonition—are we prepared?

We meet the protagonists of the mystery dramas as individuals with their destinies, who sooner or later come to a boundary in their inner lives: they feel a powerlessness that can hardly be overcome and that threatens to break them. The questions arising in them lead them, each in their own way, to the path of inner development. Sensitized by their karmic conflicts they open up to new perspectives. Neither of them can develop further now without the other. They painfully experience that important developments only happen within themselves once the other has taken a step forward. What I arrange, or develop, quietly with myself and the spirit has implications for me and the other. A foundation appears; but things are no less dramatic seeing that now I have responsibility for the other, too: developments that will fail if the other does not support me; a new kind of community. What kind of community is this that has, not only a passive but also an active interest in karma?

This relates to an atmosphere that begins to take up what Rudolf Steiner referred to repeatedly in his lectures, most fundamentally in the lecture "What Does the Angel Do in Our Astral Body?" The time has come now when we can actively grow toward this powerful activity of the angel in us and in humankind as a whole. What kind of community is this that is interested in the individual? Any resistance against it is inside us. Rudolf Steiner does not omit to mention it when he speaks about our time and its background. He widens our inner space by showing how our inner battleground is also that of spiritual beings whose aims are very different from our future possibilities. This creates tension in us.

Rudolf Steiner says that Lucifer and Ahriman are wrestling with us, not only inwardly. Although we don't notice this, they have, through us, an effect on our karmic community. Seeing through this tension and taking hold of it freely means that the inner space is more freely available. These "open spaces" also reach the community through me, and they build trust and bring order to karma.

Rudolf Steiner probably illustrated this theme most clearly in his fourth mystery drama, *The Souls' Awakening*, in the two scenes that depict the "cosmic midnight hour."

I find that viewers who have seen performances of all four dramas often forget these two scenes, or they don't remember them because they actually fell asleep. Afterward, one speaks about Johannes, Capesius, and so on, but rarely about the "cosmic midnight hour." It passes us by—so very remote, so incomprehensible, so intricate...

These scenes are about the stage in life after death that is still deeply unconscious for us today: where we arrive once we have passed through many different spheres. Having gathered experiences in the various planetary spheres, we proceed to evermore distant realms, from Moon to Saturn. Rudolf Steiner has described them all in his lectures. The scenes we will look at today are about the spheres where souls from a past incarnation meet: the spheres of Sun and Saturn. The souls are unable to experience the spheres from the Sun to Mars to Jupiter to Saturn in a wakeful state. They are guided there by Lucifer.

Some souls, who have prepared themselves on Earth by undergoing inner training and consciously absorbing certain impulses, awaken at this stage and not only work through past experiences there but make conscious decisions for their next incarnation. In the mystery drama we witness how the members of a karmic community that was together in the Middle Ages meet in this sphere and how they perceive each other. We meet them as the protagonists who have been introduced to us and who are taking hold of their destiny. This is never, ever, without transformation. What were they like in their last incarnation? Some were solitary, others members of groups that were hostile to each other and unable to maintain a familial relationship.

After death, in the moment of the greatest overview—not only over the most recent but over many past lives—we see how the souls overcome their enmities, fears, and so on, and how, as they make new decisions, they weave a new fabric. They need to forget this; it must not be present in their later day-consciousness, but it works unconsciously. If we take in these images from the mystery dramas and deepen them further, an important insight emerges, which will later be able to effect a complete transformation free from any coercion: we will be able to anticipate before death what otherwise only happens after death and, as a consequence, leave a different karmic footprint.

We will now look at an extract from scene 6 of *The Souls' Awakening*. We are in the sphere of Saturn where the soul of Capesius is waking up. He is in conversation with a soul he knows from his last life, a soul that helps him and knows him almost better than he knows himself. Their conversation is about the souls he longs to follow or that stir him; they awaken all his spirit scruples and even "burn" him. The consultation helps him to overcome his yearning and focus on his own progress; on the other hand, he decides to approach a soul in the future that he had considered unimportant in the past. The decision is painful, however. Capesius hears words spoken that he had addressed to this soul in their past life, but he hears it *from the other's mouth.* The words burn in his soul and are transformed into the impulse to seek out that soul.

CAPESIUS' SOUL

O how this penitent bewilders me.
His rays of soul pierce burningly the sheaths
of my own soul.—Thus souls work actively
beholding inmost depths of other souls.

FELIX BALDE'S SOUL (in a hollow, somewhat veiled voice)

My worthy Kean—you have been ever faithful.

CAPESIUS' SOUL

Myself—they were my very words—from him—
as echo sounding forth in spirit realms—
This is the soul I am compelled to seek.
He knows me well—through him I'll find myself.[1]

In our next example we see transformation, not of only one person. We witness a conversation being perceived by three other souls. For them, the situation becomes an example of how souls live and work for one another: empathic, active soul chemistry in wisdom and love. This is not abstract wisdom; Theodora is active in it. Active love is at work in Felicia; both endeavor to mitigate Felix's isolation.

The souls of the deceased Knights Templar observe the women's meeting. They reveal themselves as working on each other. The first sees the image and draws a lesson from it. The second is next to him, informing him that he will always be with him so that, thanks to his tenderness, he can see the image that presents itself in that moment. The third, standing behind them, also sees the image and helps the first two to enter it, so that they can not only see the figures, but even hear them speak. He lends them the power to explore what they see from the inside so that it can speak to them. The three faculties intermingle, and only then an image of the future emerges.

ROMANUS' SOUL

Two souls are drawing near the penitent,
ahead of them the spirit whom the souls
will always choose through love to be their guide.
The soul ahead rays out a tender light
that flows into the other, nearing, too,
as penitent. The vision radiates
the glow of beauty living here as wisdom.

TORQUATUS' SOUL (a figure visible only from the chest up, with blue aura, green wings)

You see the afterglow of longing's light
that I ray forth from my soul sheaths upon
your sphere in loyal spirit brotherhood.
The powers of destiny assigned to me
the task of stirring gentleness in you.
If spirit souls can serve each other thus.
Out of itself, your stern, unbending mind
would never find the life-gift of compassion.

BELLICOSUS' SOUL (a figure like Torquatus' Soul, but with blue-violet aura and blue-green wings.)

Find strength to hear in spirit—there is speaking
the soul that radiates the light of mildness
and Saturn's glory draws from out these souls
the shining glow of spirit blissfulness.

....

ROMANUS' SOUL

We have beheld within this spirit orb
the word of love and word of action join
themselves, and this will strengthen in ourselves
the seeds we'll need in future life on Earth.[2]

The next extract is from the end of the sojourn in the Saturn sphere, where the transformation takes hold of the individual's will and destiny. Here, a soul faces the situation of having to make a sacrifice for another soul. It realizes through new insights that another soul drifted into the sphere of Lucifer through its fault. Lucifer now mirrors this back to it. In its past life this soul was a devoted monk who had fallen into bitter opposition to the Knights' Order. It is consumed with hatred and condemnation.

From *The Trials of the Soul*, scene 7:

MONK (alone)

O that my office forces me to enter
the hall of this most hateful Order.
On every side my eye encounters
these devilish designs and sinful images.
An agonizing horror grips me...
It's crackling—O it's rumbling through the hall;
I feel how evil powers want to encircle me...

....

As I am not aware of any sin,
I bid defiance to the adversaries
O...the horror grows.

....

(*The Spirit of Benedictus appears.*)

All good spirits, stand by me now![3]

In this moment of despair, his deceased master appears to him. In a trance-like vision he receives his master's counsel to see the Templar Knights as *brothers* when contemplating the distant future.

BENEDICTUS

...and only when our brothers' aims
unite for peaceful purposes
with those the heretics pursue,

can good in earthly progress blossom forth.[4]

This future image, which the deceased beholds, is communicated to a soul that is still alive, and it changes and widens the scope of knowledge and actions of this soul's present life. The individual can achieve this change of soul even if he is not yet able to live it.

From *The Trials of the Soul*, scene 9:

Monk

...I know that I will find you, noble power[5]

The monk (an earlier incarnation of Maria) has attained on Earth what is commonly not attained until after death and what can usually only be realized in a subsequent incarnation. Maria went through this transformation in her earthly life, but this did not affect her karmic compass, which remained unchanged.

Maria manages (in her incarnation as a monk) to question and ultimately overcome her hatred and prejudice. Before that, however, she created an almost insurmountable distance between a son and his father; the son was a pupil who was close to her, and the father she took for a dangerous heretic. The consequences will affect her future lives. The division of father and son she now experiences as her own separation from Johannes. The hatred she built up in the past life gave Lucifer the power to create a distance between Thomas (Johannes in the later life) and Maria. Through the distance from the father, Lucifer was able to promote a sense of independence in Thomas that now unfolds its full effect.

We see how Lucifer made use of the enemy image instilled by the monk in Thomas' soul in his medieval incarnation.

This now works against the monk. This enemy image has to become a hostile force in the next life that makes Johannes turn against Maria, the reincarnated monk. Maria now experiences the error committed in her earlier life as flames burning within her. Her former great error has caused this turn of events. Now something is burning. Something does not yet appear in the light of calmness and tranquility but through restless inner flames. It appears in Maria's soul in a moment of immense powerlessness.

Johannes experiences a spiritual dilemma in his present life, and he calls into the spiritual world. Benedictus, the spiritual teacher, and Maria both hear him and they have to respond. Maria feels flames within herself that drag her thinking to the remote place where Johannes is. There, her thinking struggles.

From *The Souls' Awakening*, scene 4:

BENEDICTUS

So sounds from ever empty fields of ice
the friend's entreating call in cosmic reaches.

MARIA

The cold of ice is *burning* in my Self,
enkindling tongues of flame in my soul depths;
the flames consume the power of my thinking.

BENEDICTUS

In depths of your own soul the fire blazes.
Johannes kindles it in cosmic frost.

MARIA

The flames are fleeing—fleeing with my thinking;
....
And there at distant cosmic shores of soul

a furious battle—my own thinking fights—
at flowing nothingness—cold spirit light—
my thinking wavers, reels—cold light—it strikes
out of my thinking flaming waves of darkness—
what now emerges from the fierce, dark heat?
my Self storms, flaming red—into the light—
into cold light—of world fields of ice.[6]

Maria, a spiritually advanced soul, undergoes an experience of which we know through Rudolf Steiner; in the moment of greatest powerlessness—if this is consciously experienced—the reality of the cosmic midnight hour can shine through.

Rudolf Steiner demonstrates how the *fleeing* flames of scene 4 now *approach* her in scene 6, in the cosmic midnight hour. She has the same experience in the spirit sphere, but reversed. With Johannes—guided by Lucifer—the flames confront her.

Now, in the sphere of Saturn, we have a comprehensive vision. We experience with Maria how her transformed thinking fights with her erroneous thinking in Johannes' soul and how she fights against Lucifer in Johannes. Through the Guardian, who reveals to Maria what her task is, we see her enormous responsibility, which only she can now resolve in the cosmic midnight hour. All unresolved forces from the past appear as thunderstorms around Maria. At this hour she must make a decision regarding her and Johannes' future. She makes the difficult decision not to continue her further development with Benedictus without Johannes. Johannes' future development is tied to Lucifer and has so far not been karmically connected with Benedictus—the change is effected by her alone. Maria makes the decision and all is calm: the Guardian accepts her decision. With this promise the cosmic lightning and thunder fade away.

From *The Souls' Awakening*, scene 6:

MARIA'S SOUL

The flames are nearing—nearing with my thinking
from distant cosmic soul-shores of my being.—
A heated battle nears—and my own thinking
must battle with the thoughts of Lucifer;
within another soul my thinking fights.—
Hot light is wafted—out of fierce dark coldness.—
It flashes lightnings, this hot light of soul—
the light of soul—in cosmic fields of ice—

LUCIFER

Perceive this light—hot cosmic light of mine—
Behold the lightnings, striking your own thinking—
they strike from Lucifer's *domains of power*.
Across the bounds of your horizon here
as you perceive the cosmic midnight hour,
I bring the soul so closely bound to you.
In future you must change your searching path
if you desire the closeness to this soul.
And you, O soul, now following me, use here
the forces of the light that's raying forth
by Saturn on her cosmic midnight hour.

....

[Johannes appears]

....

MARIA'S SOUL

So let within world light my words grow strong
which at this cosmic midnight I entrust
unto the soul that Lucifer has brought.
All that is dear to me in depths of soul,
I will behold it and, beholding, speak
and, speaking, form a tone within his soul
that he, perceiving it again on Earth,

brings lovingly to life within his being.
What do I see now in my inmost core?
A holy, flaming script shines forth to me.
My love is flaming toward that teacher-soul
who guided me on Earth, who guided me
in spirit constantly from age to age,
who always found me, when in earthly danger
my ardent prayer besought his help, although
he dwelt in spirit heights; in radiant brightness
this love appears to me. Sound forth, you word
of love, from me now to the other soul.

....

What flames awaken with that word of love?
They glow so gently; from their gentleness
streams lofty earnestness, while wisdom's lightnings
with grace are flashing through the cosmic ether,
and blissfulness, while weaving joy, streams forth
to fill the wide horizon of my soul.
O, everlasting time, I do entreat you,
pour out yourself into this blissfulness
and let the teacher, let the other soul
abide with me within you, peace-imbued.

The Guardian

So shall the lightnings melt now into naught,
that dazzling shine on the Necessities,
when wakeful souls live through the cosmic North.
And thunder lose its rumbling, rolling tone
of warning at the cosmic midnight hour.

....

Johannes' Soul

Into my soul's horizon moves—this star—
it shines forth blissfulness—it glows with grace—
a star of soul within world ether—floating—

....

and there—in feeble light, a second star—
though soft it sounds, I'll hear the words it speaks.

SPIRIT OF JOHANNES' YOUTH

I feed with life your wishes very being.
My breath will pour into your youthful aims
illumining strength when worlds begin to tempt
whereto I joyfully can be your guide.
But should you lose me in yourself, I must
fall victim to the shades, bereft of being.
O blossom of my life—do not forsake me.

LUCIFER

Forsake you, he will not. I can perceive
desires for light within his depths, desires
which stray away far from the other's path.
If these desires, with self-engendered glory,
take root as Being deep within his soul,
they will bear fruit, but what they have to bear
he will not wish to waste within the realm
where love holds sway, but love deprived of beauty.[7]

Maria's decision is a challenge to Lucifer; this opposition takes effect in Johannes. But she sees that she is the cause, and she accepts her own and Johannes' destiny.

The mystery dramas illustrate how we work on the other's divinity before birth and how this is a blessing for one's own and for the other's destiny. What does this mean for the development of a community, of our Society? The protagonists' narratives break off after the fourth drama. The sphere of the cosmic midnight hour waits to be absorbed in each individual, as an archetype of community, down into the individual decision to change, to take responsibility.

The idea of reincarnation has spread far and wide over the past century. Knowing that I will return makes a difference.

The cosmic midnight hour shows how very closely the thought of reincarnation is connected with karmic relationships, be they with friends or opponents. I live in the other, the other lives in me; we build our future together. What would happen if we were able *now* to have something of this "night experience" in our daytime consciousness?

6. The Evolving Body of the Anthroposophical Society

Marc Desaules

Dear friends, the spiritual-scientific movement founded by Rudolf Steiner—with those who directly or indirectly relate to or are inspired by it—is, to my knowledge, the only one among the multitude of spiritual movements in our time that speaks not only of a spiritual world, but also of the threshold between the sensory and the suprasensory worlds, and in particular of the guardian of that threshold, who admonishes us to beware of the dangers awaiting the human soul as it crosses this threshold. This particular feature of the anthroposophical movement is, as we will see, a response to a change in humanity's spiritual situation that began in the nineteenth century and became fully effective during World War I. The newly founded Anthroposophical Society, as the home of the growing anthroposophical movement, can be seen as a necessary consequence of this change.

What happened? During this period of time the relationship of human beings with the spiritual world changed completely. We could say that the soul no longer has its center of gravity in the sensory but in the spiritual world. The soul experiences the spiritual world as a reality that is directly adjacent to our ordinary consciousness but remains subliminal, unconscious, because we are still lacking the concepts to consciously take hold of it. This is an inversion of orientation that will have consequences. For the soul it will in future be less about finding the way to the spirit in order to be nurtured by it—this is something humanity has already achieved—but about getting to know and understand the differences between the experiences it has on this side of the threshold, in the world of the senses, and those it has beyond the threshold, in the spiritual world. Anthroposophy has devoted much attention to this threshold, this abyss of the human soul, and to its guardian, from Rudolf Steiner's first writings of 1904[1] on how to attain knowledge of the higher worlds to the esoteric lessons of the first class of the School for Spiritual Science. Rudolf Steiner placed particular emphasis on the gravity of this topic in his concluding lecture, on January 1, 1924, at the Christmas Conference,[2] during which the Anthroposophical Society was newly founded.

He repeatedly described this new development as the crossing of the threshold by humanity as a whole, for instance, in April 1919:

> It is in our era that humanity, as a whole, has to cross a threshold. Not everyone needs to be conscious of this crossing. If, for instance, the majority of people continue to think as they do today, if they continue to reject spiritual knowledge, then humanity will cross the threshold, but hardly anyone would be aware of it. This powerful experience of spirit and soul, which we can describe as crossing the threshold, will only be conscious to those who

> are open to the knowledge imparted by Spiritual Science. But even if no one notices that humanity is actually in the process of crossing this threshold, it is still a reality. Such an event in human evolution does not depend on whether or not people are aware of it.[3]

He described the situation even more precisely in 1924:

> There is a real abyss.... In crossing this abyss, human beings have actually crossed a threshold. A guardian stands at this threshold. Initially, humankind was unable to notice him as it went past him between 1842 and 1879. But for its own salvation it now has to look back and observe the guardian. Not taking notice of him and continuing to live through the next centuries without taking notice of him would be utterly devastating for humankind.[4]

This change—which became fully effective in 1917[5]—is more radical than it seems, and its implications for the social and individual life are of a dimension we can hardly foresee. Rudolf Steiner's active promotion of the threefold social organism reflects the significance he attached to this new spiritual situation. Now is not the time nor is this the place to discuss this question in detail, but we see how everywhere around us everything—really everything to do with human coexistence—needs to be done to balance the polarities and tensions that any society faces, so that they, instead of causing evermore wars and destruction, can become fruitful sources of life.

Rudolf Steiner worked incessantly to create a social organism whereby tensions can unfold between the economic life, the life of rights, and the spiritual–cultural life, rather than between countries. The consequences of the new spiritual situation are also dramatic for individual souls. For what does it mean for them to cross the threshold unconsciously? It means that they are not able to differentiate clearly between the world of the senses and that of the spirit. They are in danger of losing their sense of reality and inner coherence. It means nothing less than forgoing the ability to know the spiritual world, because an illusionary world will take over. The anthroposophical movement has a specific role to play in this because it is the only movement that knows about this threshold, about this abyss that gapes at the frontier of the sensory world, about the guardian who watches over it, and about his appeal to us to be cautious. The anthroposophical movement bears great responsibility for the cultural future of humankind. In the lecture mentioned, Rudolf Steiner expands on this responsibility, referring us back to the founding of the Anthroposophical Society, on which he concentrates all his hopes, not only for the New Year but also for the future of a human culture on Earth.

I will emphasize the importance of this Anthroposophical Society here, though some may take exception to this because they have felt the need to distance themselves from this Society. I see the Anthroposophical Society as a vantage ground for experiencing the threshold and the guardian that is exposed and protected at the same time; a place where these realities can be grasped, understood, and practiced. This is why one becomes a member of the Anthroposophical Society. Anthroposophy alone does not provide the necessary framework. Anthroposophy is a spiritual reality that needs to incarnate in order to radiate out into our culture and become effective. For this it needs to find a sufficiently noble form, a body that allows it to become part of earthly life. In my view the Anthroposophical Society is this emerging body for Anthroposophy, where true humanity, which is what makes us what we are and distinguishes us, can be cultivated and developed, so that the human race has the chance of a future. It is of this Anthroposophical Society that I wish to speak, this Society in which Rudolf Steiner, once again shortly before his death, placed all his hopes.

That this Anthroposophical Society, this "association of people whose will it is to nurture the life of the soul, both in the individual and in human society, on the basis of a true knowledge of the spiritual world,"[6] was envisaged as a building is clear from the words spoken at its foundation. Having welcomed the members of the congress a day earlier and presented the bylaws, Rudolf Steiner opened the assembly on Christmas Day 1923, by speaking of the "foundation stone" of this new Society. He began with the three forces at work both in human beings and in the cosmos. In a presentation rich with images he invited people to use the formative substance of these forces to create a microcosmic dodecahedron as an image of the macrocosmic dodecahedron. This is how he formed what he called the "foundation stone," which he sank not into the ground but into the souls of those present. The intimate relationship of this Society with the first Goetheanum is obvious: its foundation stone, a double dodecahedron, was planted on the Dornach hill ten years earlier and is still there today. This connection is important for an understanding of the Anthroposophical Society. A week later, when the conference came to a close, this was clearly confirmed.

> My dear friends, it was a year ago yesterday that we looked upon the flames that consumed the old Goetheanum.... May we—once the physical Goetheanum stands here—have worked in such a way that it will be only an outer symbol of our spiritual Goetheanum, a symbol we will carry within us as an idea when we now go out into the world. We have laid the foundation stone here. Upon this foundation stone, a building will be raised from bricks shaped by those who work in our groups around the world. Let us now focus on this work in spirit and think of the responsibility, about which we spoke earlier: the responsibility we have for today's human being who is now standing before the guardian of the threshold.[7]

The flames have flung the forms of the first Goetheanum into the expanses of the macrocosm. But the power of these forms has not vanished with the flames. It remains present in the spirit and can again be integrated into the world and into earthly evolution through the work of all those who wish this. There is no doubt about that. We can continue to live in these forms, which are so enlightening in our time, and we can make them shine out—from a different kind of building, a social structure, of which we ourselves are the constitutive elements. The spirit that once taught through the shapes of the first Goetheanum, through the play of forms and sculpted surfaces, can now be closely felt and experienced in the structures of the Anthroposophical Society. This makes our Society a unique place of human education, a source of orientation where we wake up to the inverted spiritual situation of our time, into which we have been newly placed. We need only to know how to go about this.

Let us look more closely at these forms. Spatially, the experience of this building, which is arranged around two

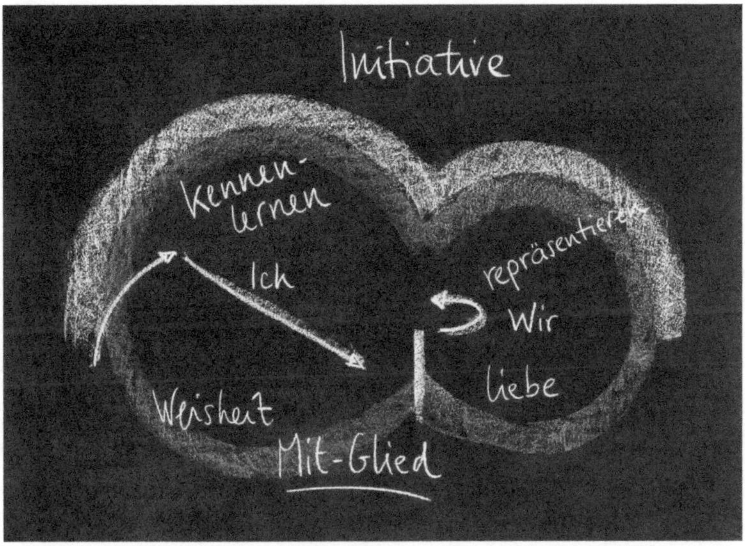

cupolas, can take us through the most subtle and fleeting soul experiences—due to its objectivity. First it engages our eye, which only has to dwell on what it sees. This building with its two intersecting domes—one larger, one smaller—has a remarkable and unique outline (see the blackboard drawing). It poses a question to its surroundings and speaks to the passerby. We go closer so that we can better observe it. The main entrance in the west is open. We walk up the stairs until we reach another portal that awakens our curiosity but that we don't just simply walk through. Turning around, we find ourselves facing the Red Window, which includes images of the threshold to the spiritual world and its guardian. It is the same with the Anthroposophical Society; when we encounter Anthroposophy and make it part of our path, we have to engage with it, and it rarely leaves people indifferent. Moreover, if the knowledge radiating from it is authentic, we might move closer, and the all-important question of becoming a member might arise in us.

The social form of this Anthroposophical Society, as described in its bylaws, is reflected in the shape of the first Goetheanum; it can be drawn as two intersecting circles, the larger of which represents the quality of the membership and corresponds to the larger dome. The smaller circle represents the quality of membership in the School for Spiritual Science and corresponds to the small cupola.

As we enter the space created by the two powerful domes the architectural forms can tell us more. Under the greater cupola is a large auditorium that slopes down toward the round, even stage area that extends below the smaller dome. Stately columns support the domes. Unlike the experience we have in a cathedral, this perspective does not invite us to stride ahead. Here—at the upper end of the main auditorium—the nearest columns are the smallest and they "grow" as the floor slopes down toward the stage. This "counter-perspective" invites us to observe. It leaves us free to find out more.

Everywhere around—in the forms of the columns, the chapters of the architraves, and the motifs engraved into the windows and painted on the vaulted ceiling—cosmic wisdom becomes tangible. In addition, there is the Anthroposophy that streams out from the stage to the auditorium. We are slowed by the need to understand. In this space, which is dedicated to Anthroposophy, knowledge is not a given; we have to want and acquire it, step by step. The quality of this space under the large cupola is best described as a gesture of "getting to know." It can be represented by an arrow that, open to new impressions, starts at the main entrance and runs toward the stage, approaching wisdom step by step (see image, page 145). The same gesture describes the membership in the Anthroposophical Society: the will to get to know

Anthroposophy in all possible forms, through study, exercises, meditation.

Learning always leads to another dimension, which can open up before us at any moment. First a sense of responsibility awakens; we begin to feel responsible for what we know. And this responsibility can grow to the point that we wish to represent this wisdom, which we have understood and internalized. It is at this point at the latest that we become aware of a boundary. A threshold appears. What is it? I give you an example: when we wish to share something of the wisdom we have acquired here, we rise from our seat, leave the space of this auditorium, and walk up the stairs that lead to the stage. What happens there? Before we begin to speak we turn around and face the auditorium. This turning around belongs to the threshold, to the transition in the stage area, the area of the small cupola.

We can illustrate this with an arrow that turns back on itself (image, page 145). This turning around is also an inner experience. Our gaze is no longer directed, searchingly, toward wisdom; now we share what we have learned. The gesture is entirely different; our wish now is to represent the knowledge we have individualized and to respond, with love, to the needs of the world and others. This quality corresponds to membership in the School for Spiritual Science, and it is no coincidence that the only condition for this membership mentioned explicitly by Rudolf Steiner is the will to be a representative of the anthroposophical cause. Understanding and realizing this condition would, as we will see later, provide the soil on which the Anthroposophical Society could grow, everywhere in the world.

The spaces underneath the two domes are clearly very different in character. Even though we breathe the same air in both of them, they represent opposite worlds that are divided by a threshold. These two worlds, or qualities, which are always in contact, never intermingle. The laws that apply on either side are not the same; they are mutually exclusive. Because the threshold is invisible we may think that it can be crossed without danger. If you step onto the stage while holding on to the attitude of the auditorium space—which is that of wanting to *get to know* Anthroposophy—you had better beware. You would continue your search without turning around and lose yourself in the wings. By carrying the laws of the auditorium onto the stage you might lose your foothold in reality. And you have to be equally careful when you leave the stage as a representative and you don't turn around and sit down. Carrying the laws of the stage area into the auditorium also creates an unwholesome situation.

This threshold experience between auditorium and stage is clearly apparent when we recall the first Goetheanum. It may seem insignificant but, in the present situation, with humanity having crossed the threshold, it is highly instructive. Are we able to understand that the qualitative difference between being a member of the Anthroposophical Society and being a member of the School for Spiritual Science lies precisely in this change of attitude between auditorium and stage, between our own search for the spiritual world and our active commitment to others in the sensory world, or even between the wish to "get to know" Anthroposophy and the wish to "be a representative" of the anthroposophical cause? For there, in our soul, we consciously experience the invisible threshold—between the sensory and the spiritual world, between the two spaces, the two qualities of membership—with its guardian who admonishes us in all earnestness to adjust our behavior to the laws that apply on either side. Here I see the most important task of the Anthroposophical Society: to become a place for this threshold experience, where we can learn to adapt our behavior to these different laws. For we already live in both worlds today.

This threshold experience can be described even more precisely. The Anthroposophical Society is a meeting place of a karmic community of people seeking to become anthroposophists. Their relationship is not an innocent one.

> You really need to know as anthroposophists that karma is harder to experience for anthroposophists than it is for others. Those who find their way to the Anthroposophical Society are predestined to a more difficult experience of karma than others. Moreover, if they try to avoid this difficult experience, if they try to have a more comfortable experience of karma, this will revenge itself in some way. You must be anthroposophists in your experience of karma, too. As true anthroposophists we must be able to look at our karma carefully. The wish for a comfortable experience of karma will revenge itself in the form of physical illness, physical accidents, and so on.[8]

Rudolf Steiner explained this further on the following day, giving us a key for overcoming this difficulty and facing our challenges.

> This is really engraved in the karma of every single anthroposophist: Be a person of initiative, and you will see—if you fail to find the center of your being with this initiative, whether because of physical hindrances or other obstacles you meet—that your joy and sorrow depend on whether or not you find your own individual initiative! This should

> stand in golden letters before the soul of every anthroposophist: initiative is part of our karma and much of what we meet in life depends on whether or not we are consciously aware of this initiative in our will.[9]

Be a person of initiative! Such a simple sentence and yet so profound. The word *initiative* encompasses much more than it seems. I will write it down here (see image, page 145).

In everyday language, we use initiative for the most intimate and vital aspect of the experiences we spoke of in relation to the threshold of the spiritual world and the guardian: for our own self, our "I." If we reflect on our journey so far—getting to know and internalizing the old wisdom of humanity and the world, connecting with the content of Rudolf Steiner's writings and lectures, being part of the anthroposophical community, or just in general—there was a particular moment when we felt the need to become involved, to do something, to take up an initiative. And if that has not happened yet, it will sooner or later. In that moment the experience of the threshold, of which we have spoken, will become an experience we are aware of and that we can practice together. Initiative is the driving force for this transition. We move on from insight to active involvement, from a cosmos of wisdom to a cosmos of love. This may be the most fundamental spiritual experience we have today; but it is so elusive that we have to learn to protect it, because it is not, and must not become, an ordinary experience. The power of this initiative is so vibrant in us once it has taken hold of our soul that we can forever be nurtured by it.

The double-domed building of the Anthroposophical Society was created for this initiative: for the transformation of the cosmos of wisdom into a cosmos of love. We need to keep returning to this truth, and become newly aware of it, so that it can gradually become a new formative principle of our Society. Up until now—and in many places this continues to be the case—titles of nobility, ties of family or blood, inherited documents of ownership, diplomas and recognized references, money or weapons, even the anonymous power of public opinion, have been authoritative principles. There is still little scope for personal initiative. In the future—if there is to be a future for humanity—individual initiative will be the main principle. Rudolf Steiner's Anthroposophical Society is the embodiment of an entirely new and revolutionary influence: a field of practice for humankind. It is like a vessel that receives and protects this process, an experimental garden that allows it to grow and unfold for a future humanity. One of the first consequences of this process is that it helps to bring order to human relationships: "*What unites the members of the Anthroposophical Society? It is the wish to put their karma in order!*"[10]

We must also look at the Anthroposophical Society in its formal environment, in the sphere of rights. It is a sphere that today, understandably, often evokes rejection or mistrust. But it is also an important aspect of incarnation. Incidentally, it is also of some significance that the Anthroposophical Society received its legal form under Swiss law. The law in Switzerland is quite unique. It allows for a degree of suppleness and differentiation that makes it possible, particularly for associations, to assume a legal form that can be adapted to almost any objective, because the main aspect is human interaction, while the written document is just a complementary formality. For those who deal with it regularly, this law is surprisingly clear and simple, especially if one compares it with the paperwork and formalities required elsewhere. It is certainly an environment that is akin to the ideas behind the Anthroposophical Society.

The fact that the Anthroposophical Society has assumed a legal form is significant in another sense, too. To understand this significance, we need to know something about the origin of the legal sphere. Let us therefore look back to the time when the question of rights first emerged. The Romans were the first to assign a legal quality to human beings. They added a legal body to the physical body: the individual or Roman citizen. Before that, the physical body had been an object of the law, as criminals were maimed according to the severity of their crime; those unable to pay their debts were handed over to their creditors, who could deal with them however they saw fit, perhaps by selling them or condemning them to slavery.

According to Rudolf Steiner, this came about because of the Romans' increasing identification with material reality. He sees it in relation to the possibility of understanding the Mystery of Golgotha. This mystery could have gone unnoticed had the Romans not created this mirror image of the human being in the legal sphere, because this was the precondition for the ability to accept the idea of the divine principle becoming flesh.

> In the art of the Greek period human beings created a world of gods in their own image. They did the same with the state. They reached an understanding of matter to the point that they united maya and the spirit. It was the moment when humanity first acquired a concept of personality. You will understand that it was also the time when human beings were able to comprehend God as a

> personal manifestation, when the spirit of the Earth, too, was able to manifest as a personality.... Human beings moved on from feeling that they were part of God to experiencing themselves as personalities. And they could even understand the idea of God as a personality who had come down to live in the flesh among them. This is why Christ Jesus appeared in that period of human evolution.[11]

Shortly after, Rudolf Steiner summed up the same situation from a different angle.

> The time when human beings had become one with the outer reality was the only period conducive to the understanding that God can incarnate as a human being. This would not have been possible at any earlier point in time: gods were considered too high and lofty then to appear in human form.[12]

The sphere of rights was clearly essential for human beings to receive the greatest event in Earth's evolution: the incarnation of the divine in a human body.

From then on, the understanding of rights evolved in parallel with individual consciousness. Up until the last third of the nineteenth century, people who organized themselves into groups were seen as individual persons, who were, as individuals, legally and financially responsible for their groups. This changed after the 1880s, in the course of only a few decades, when communities—in the form of associations, foundations, and other organizations—were assigned legal personhood, with all the rights and duties this entailed. In Switzerland the first code of law for societies dates back to 1881. The civil code defining this legislation in more detail and providing a framework for associations and foundations goes back to 1907. In Germany the civil code was accepted by the Reichstag in 1896; in France it became possible to form trade unions in 1884 and charitable associations in 1901. It is similar in most other countries. It was only about a hundred years ago that a new category of social entities was created, vested with the same rights as physical persons. These associations can make decisions, act, buy and sell, sue and defend themselves in court. With the exception of a few rights reserved exclusively to individuals (such as the civic rights to marry, have children, and so on), these associations are like individuals whose body is not, however, constituted of flesh and blood, but of bylaws that specify their name, objectives, organs, and functions. Although they have the same rights, they do not have the same spatial or temporal limitations. Their body can be spread across the Earth, and they can exist beyond a human lifetime.

This development has generated an immense challenge. Like the sorcerer's apprentice in Goethe's poem, humanity has artificially created a great number of trading companies, foundations, and associations, which were not expected to become places of incarnation for beings that gradually developed a dynamic of their own: for this more recent development in the legal sphere—the invention of the juristic person—occurred at the same time as the spiritual change of 1879, referred to by Rudolf Steiner as "the descent of the spirits of darkness," with the corresponding consequences affecting humankind in the following centuries. It seems likely that there is a connection and that during that period, when these beings from the spiritual world were cast to the Earth, the sphere of rights was twisted or distorted in order to receive them and provide the means for their future actions. In 1905 Rudolf Steiner spoke from an entirely different perspective of an important phenomenon that is evoked by people working together in groups: "*People working together in fraternities are like magicians because they attract higher beings.... This is the mystery of progress for future humanity: to work together as communities.*"[13] Where is the difference? We will come back to that.

We know about the long evolutionary path of the individual, whose physical form has organized and refined itself so as to become able to receive the spark of consciousness and gain self-awareness. It is a purifying of cognitive and instinctive activity, so that from between these two poles—thinking and will—a rhythm could emerge that gives space alternately to the one and the other, without either of them ever gaining the upper hand. This permanent striving for balance may well be an expression of the noblest quality that characterizes the human being. This "becoming human" relied, however, on the model of a physical body received in a key moment two thousand years ago. How is it with groups? The fact is that groups are recognized as juristic persons, whether or not that makes sense.[14]

Do groups then not also need a model? There is no doubt in my view that their bylaw-bodies need to be ennobled and humanized if humanity is not to head for social disaster. Like individual human beings, communities need a model for their development. That model is the form created by Rudolf Steiner and the members of the Christmas Conference of 1923/1924 as the Anthroposophical Society—a form that any group of people can strive to copy in order to appeal to the higher selves of its constituents rather than allow brute instincts to hold sway. People are better or worse depending on the structures they give themselves, and the quality of an organization depends less on the individual values of its constituents than on its organizational form. We also need to be clear about the fact that the space taken up by the countless societies, foundations, and associations in the world has by now become so extensive that this space will be where the future of humanity is decided.

We have seen that the form of the Anthroposophical Society is a copy of the architectural structure of the first Goetheanum, with its intersecting polar spaces that can develop a dialog in their own rhythm. This essential gesture, which is that of the human form, is revealed in the building as an open secret. We have also seen how these spaces evoke diametrically opposed soul experiences, depending on whether you are in the auditorium or on stage. We find these experiences reflected in the structure of the Anthroposophical Society, with the different qualities of membership in the Society or in the School for Spiritual Science. There again we see the same mystery of the human form. We see how this Society assumed its physical manifestation at Christmas 1923, as a result of Rudolf Steiner's initiative and suggestions on the one hand and the affirmation and support of those attending the conference on the other. The bylaws were presented and discussed item by item, down to the financial implications. Rudolf Steiner proposed to extend the initiative to include an executive council, a suggestion that the members present greeted with applause. It is an essential aspect of the emerging Society that there was no vote; the process of appointing the Council members is not mentioned with a single word in the bylaws.[15]

It was a model gathering, free, wished for by both sides, between the initiative and what I would call the acceptance of this initiative by others, between those who took on responsibility and those who supported them, without either side claiming a position of power. The same gesture was extended to the institution of the School for Spiritual Science and the responsibility spread across its Sections. The principle of *initiative* was the only one ever applied here. The gesture continued after the conference, when Rudolf Steiner invited those members who wished to be representatives of the anthroposophical cause to become members of the School for Spiritual Science and bear responsibility for the future of Anthroposophy *alongside him.* The form that the first Goetheanum assumed in space was assumed by the Anthroposophical Society in the sphere of rights. We see before us the archetype of a juristic form that is the most perfect expression of human community-building.

Just as two thousand years ago, this act would have been meaningless had it already occurred. It was necessary to wait until groups of people attained the status of legal personhood—in other words, until groups were granted the same rights and obligations that individuals have. Will these associations be places where fallen higher beings will incarnate and impose their will on us, or will they be places where the initiative of some, supported by the recognition of others, will attract higher beings? Only in the latter case will the associations serve human evolution on Earth. Humanity has a new task: it needs to educate human societies. This great task is like a reflection of the crossing of the threshold by humanity as a whole. The Anthroposophical Society is the masterpiece created by Rudolf Steiner and his followers at this crucial point of development to integrate into the world of human communities the model of a (legal) person, which will be moral because it is constituted in the image of the human being.

Individuals refer to themselves as "I," and groups as "we." When a group of individuals become a single person (an innovative element added in the last third of the nineteenth century), that person has a higher kind of identity; it is a kind of larger "I." This person cannot speak of itself in the first person singular. It needs a worthy representative to speak on its behalf. This representative will speak of "we," no longer to referring to the individuals united in this society, but as the representative of a higher identity. It is the same word but it reflects a fuller kind of responsibility. For those who understand this there is a subtle but definite difference; it can never be "I." This quality again illustrates the difference between the two spaces (see image, page 145); on the one side we are individuals ("I"), on the other representatives ("we"). The higher identity opens another dimension, one where the spiritual world and its beings are present and active, as well as the dead, who are close to us and beings of the higher hierarchies.

We now have this image of the Anthroposophical Society as a double-domed building, regained from the vestiges left by the flames that consumed the first Goetheanum. We understand it as a place devoted to the initiative and to the acceptance of this initiative; between the two is the experience of the threshold and of the guardian that we need to get to know if we are not to lose our humanity once humankind as a whole has crossed the threshold. I repeat the words spoken by Rudolf Steiner that I cited earlier, with particular emphasis on the fact that they relate to working in groups:

"We have laid the foundation stone here. On this foundation stone a building will be raised from bricks shaped by those who are at work in our groups around the world."[16]

Each stone of the building symbolizes the work done in the groups. We have too narrow a concept of these groups when we think of only the branches that exist around the world. I don't think that was Rudolf Steiner's image. Any union of active individuals anywhere in the world, as long as it is formed according to the example of the Anthroposophical Society—i.e., around the active involvement of those who carry the initiative and represent the anthroposophical cause, as well as those who gather around and acknowledge that initiative because there they find what they are striving for—is such a group.

Whenever such a group forms, it becomes an expression of the Goetheanum and contributes locally to building the body of the Anthroposophical Society—through closeness, directly, wherever Anthroposophy is represented and recognized, here or there, anywhere on Earth. Consider a biodynamic farm. Latently, it is already this society, and the farmer is implicitly a member of the School for Spiritual Science, because he or she represents anthroposophic agriculture; its clients and friends are implicit members of the Society, because a thirst for biodynamic ideas and methods draws them to that farm. The same is true for Waldorf schools; teachers have the initiative and the responsibility for such teaching as *de facto* members of the School for Spiritual Science; they represent anthroposophical education in the world, which gives direction to the parents who come to the school with their children, because they find something there that answers a need in their souls as *de facto* members of the Society. Again, those two qualities come together. Or a medical practice in which a physician promotes anthroposophic medicine and where patients arrive for a particular treatment. In each anthroposophical initiative, we see the same crucial gesture—the meeting of two realms—and the archetypal form of the Anthroposophical Society, manifested in the world as a double-domed building.

This is no utopia. I am convinced that we can realize the impulse of the Christmas Conference of 1923 on the basis of such an image and give the Anthroposophical Society the possibility to gradually become the body of the anthroposophical movement. For this reason, we must give up the current, misleading idea of an Anthroposophical Society with the School for Spiritual Science as a kind of sacred precinct at the top and the areas of applied Anthroposophy below. This way of thinking belongs to the time before the Christmas Conference, before the "act of consecration" that marked the "beginning of the turning point of time,"[17] to cite Rudolf Steiner. It is based on an esotericism[18] that needed protection of a different sort before 1917 than it has required since then. Today we must learn to think the reality—which is sensory and spiritual at the same time—in concepts relating to the Goetheanum, the double-domed building, and to discover there the threefoldness that is expressed in the interacting polarity that is devoted to the mystery of the threshold and of the guardian. The Anthroposophical Society itself will then become the archetype that reveals this mystery, which is also the mystery of the human being, in each of its activities.

We need courage to make space in our hearts and minds for this emerging body that is the Anthroposophical Society and we need courage to rid ourselves of certain preconceptions that continue to veil the reality that awaits us: "*We will look to this work in spirit and be aware of the responsibility we spoke of today for the modern human being who is standing before the guardian of the threshold.*" We can gain awareness of this responsibility and the Goetheanum spirit today by looking at the work of the groups. The good spirit of the Goetheanum (which we can see as the guardian of the threshold) manifests and can be perceived wherever anthroposophists are active in the world. Then we will be able to offer fertile ground to the good spirit of the Goetheanum:

Light divine,
Sun of Christ,
Give warmth to our hearts;
Enlighten our heads;

That good may become
What from our hearts
we are founding,
what from our heads
we direct
with single purpose.[19]

Notes

Preface

1 Rudolf Steiner, *Die Weihnachtstagung zur Begründung der Allgemeinen Anthroposophischen Gesellschaft 1923/24*. CW 260. Dornach 1994, p. 281 [in English: *The Christmas Conference: For the Foundation of the General Anthroposophical Society, 1923/1924* (Anthroposophic Press, 1990)].

1. Existential Relationships with the Anthroposophical Society

1 Otfried Dörfler, «Zum Geleit». In *Elisabeth Vreede. 1879–1943. Mitteilungen aus dem anthroposophischen Leben in der Schweiz*, special issue 7. Christmas 2003, p. 8 [in English: *Elisabeth Vreede: Adversity, Resilience, and Spiritual Science* (SteinerBooks, 2017)].

2 Otfried Dörfler, «Zum Geleit». In *Besinnung auf Maria Ita Wegman. Die treue Mitarbeiterin Rudolf Steiners. Die geistige Kämpferin für eine michaelische Zukunft. Die Mitbegründerin des anthroposophisch erweiterten medizinschen Impulses. Mitteilungen aus dem anthroposophischen Leben in der Schweiz,* special issue 5. Christmas 1997, p. 8.

3 Rudolf Steiner, *Mysteriengestaltungen*. CW 232. Dornach 1998, p. 225 [in English: *Mystery Knowledge and Mystery Centers* (Rudolf Steiner Press, 1973)].

4 Rudolf Steiner, *The Guardian of the Threshold*, p. 117, tr. R. and H. Pusch [in English: *Four Mystery Dramas* (SteinerBooks, 2014)].

5 Ibid.

6 Rudolf Steiner, *Erfahrungen des Übersinnlichen. Die drei Wege der Seele zu Christus*. CW 143. Dornach 1994, p. 233.

7 Cited in Ulrich Häussermann, *Friedensfeier. Eine Einführung in Hölderlins Christushymnen*. Arlesheim 2010, p. 37.

8 Ibid., p. 44.

9 Albert Steffen, *Geistesschulung und Gemeinschaftsbildung*. Dornach 1974, p. 74.

10 In Marie Steiner, *Rudolf Steiner und die redenden Künste. Gesammelte Schriften II*. Dornach 1974, p. 32.

11 Hella Wiesberger (ed.), *Marie Steiner: Briefe und Dokumente, vornehmlich aus ihrem letzten Lebensjahr*. Dornach 1991, p. 230. (Marie Steiner, Letters and Documents, mostly from the last year of her life)

12 Goetheanum Archives. Cf. Uwe Werner, «Über das Archiv habe ich nie gesprochen.» In *Elisabeth Vreede. 1879–1943. Mitteilungen aus dem anthroposophischen Leben in der Schweiz*, special issue 7, p. 83.

13 Sergei O. Prokofieff, *Warum wird man Mitglied der Anthroposophischen Gesellschaft?* Dornach 2011, p. 9 [in English: *Why Become a Member of the Anthroposophical Society?* (Temple Lodge, 2012)].

14 Rudolf Steiner, *Anthroposophische Gemeinschaftsbildung*. CW 257. Dornach 1989, p. 120 [in English: *Awakening to Community* (SteinerBooks, 1975)].

15 Albert Steffen, *Buch der Rückschau*. Dornach 1976, p. 174.

16 Hella Wiesberger (ed.), *Marie Steiner: Briefe und Dokumente, vornehmlich aus ihrem letzten Lebensjahr*, p. 254.

17 Ibid., p. 359.

18 Ibid., p. 20.

19 Rudolf Steiner, *Die Geschichte und die Bedingungen der anthroposophischen Bewegung im Verhältnis zur Anthroposophischen Gesellschaft*. CW 258. Dornach 1981, p. 120 [in English: *The Anthroposophic Movement* (Rudolf Steiner Press, 1993)].

20 Rudolf Steiner, *Mein Lebensgang*. CW 28. Dornach 2000, p. 411 [in English: *Autobiography: Chapters in the Course of My Life, 1861–1907* (SteinerBooks, 2000)].

21 Marie von Sivers' letter to Édouard Schuré of Oct. 7, 1905. Cited in Hella Wiesberger, *Marie Steiner-von Sivers. Ein Leben für die Anthroposophie*. Dornach 1989, p. 116.

22 Rudolf Steiner / Marie Steiner-von Sivers, *Briefwechsel und Dokumente. 1901–1925*. CW 262. Dornach 2002, p. 154 [in English: *Correspondence and Documents 1901–1925* (Anthroposophic Press, 1988)].

23 Cited in Marie Savitch, *Marie Steiner-von Sivers. Mitarbeiterin Rudolf Steiners*. Dornach 1965, p. 96f.

24 Rudolf Steiner, *Mantrische Sprüche. Seelenübungen*, vol. 2. CW 268. Dornach 1999, p. 290 [in English: *Soul Exercises: Word*

and Symbol Meditations, 1903–1924 (SteinerBooks, 2015)]. See also Peter Selg, *Michael als Genius der Zivilisationsentwicklung. Rudolf Steiners Abschied von Berlin*. Arlesheim 2013, p. 50f.

25 Rudolf Steiner, cited in Hella Wiesberger, *Marie Steiner von Sivers. Ein Leben für die Anthroposophie,* p. 473.

26 Rudolf Steiner / Marie Steiner-von Sivers, *Briefwechsel und Dokumente. 1901–1925*. CW 262, p. 361 [in English: *Correspondence and Documents 1901–1925* (Anthroposophic Press, 1988)].

27 Rudolf Steiner, *Die Konstitution der Allgemeinen Anthroposophischen Gesellschaft und der Freien Hochschule für Geisteswissenschaft. Der Wiederaufbau des Goetheanums*. CW 260a. Dornach 1987, p. 110.

28 Marie Steiner-von Sivers' letter to Ehrenfried Pfeiffer of Sept. 15, 1948. In Marie Steiner, *Briefe und Dokumente,* p. 309.

29 Marie Steiner-von Sivers' letter to Olga von Freymann of Sept. 19, 1948. Ibid., p. 354ff.

30 In Christian Morgenstern, *Ein Leben in Briefen*. Ed. Margareta Morgenstern. Wiesbaden 1952, p. 481f (corrected based on Morgenstern's manuscript). On the context of this letter cf. Peter Selg, *Christian Morgenstern. Sein Weg mit Rudolf Steiner.* Stuttgart 2013, p. 259ff.

31 Marie Steiner-von Sivers' letter to Ehrenfried Pfeiffer of July 15, 1948. In *Marie Steiner. Briefe und Dokumente*, p. 282 (author's emphasis).

32 Marie Steiner-von Sivers' letter to Ehrenfried Pfeiffer of Jan. 6, 1948. Ibid., p. 236.

33 Marie Steiner-von Sivers' letter to Richard Dürich of Sept. 3, 1947. Ibid., p. 334.

34 Ibid., p. 330.

35 Marie Steiner-von Sivers, «Über den Fall Tomberg». Undated note, circa 1936. Ibid., p. 326.

36 Marie Steiner-von Sivers' letter to Helga Geelmuyden of July 21, 1948. Ibid., p. 353.

37 Marie Steiner-von Sivers' letter to Ehrenfried Pfeiffer of Jan. 6, 1948. Ibid., p. 231.

38 Marie Steiner-von Sivers' letter to a Christian Community priest of March 30, 1948. Ibid., p. 351.

39 Marie Steiner-von Sivers' letter to Richard Dürich of Sept. 3, 1947. Ibid., p. 339.

40 Marie Steiner-von Sivers' letter of Jan. 25, 1946. Ibid., p. 212.

41 Marie Steiner-von Sivers' letter to Ehrenfried Pfeiffer of Jan. 6, 1948. Ibid., p. 234.

42 Marie Steiner-von Sivers, «An die Mitglieder der Anthroposophischen Gesellschaft in der Schweiz». In *Nachrichtenblatt*, vol. 19, no. 51. Dec. 20, 1942.

43 «Welches sind die Aufgaben des Nachlassvereins?» (July 1945). In Marie Steiner, *Briefe und Dokumente*, p. 192.

44 Ibid., p. 198.

45 Fred Poeppig, *Marie Steiner. Ein Leben im Dienst der Wiedergeburt des Wortes*. Basel 1949, p. 141.

46 Marie Savitch, *Marie Steiner-von Sivers. Mitarbeiterin Rudolf Steiners*, p. 191.

47 Rudolf Steiner, *Truth-Wrought-Words: With Other Verses and Prose Passages*, CW 40. Anthroposophic Press 1979, p. 29.

48 In Madeleine P. van Deventer and Elisabeth Knottenbelt (eds.), *Elisabeth Vreede. Ein Lebensbild*. Arlesheim 1976, p. 110f.

49 *Ita Wegman und die Anthroposophie. Ein Gespräch mit Emanuel Zeylmans*. Flensburger Hefte, special issue 17. Flensburg 1996, p. 34f [in English: *Ita Wegman and Anthroposophy: A Conversation with Emanuel Zeylmans* (SteinerBooks, 2012)].

50 In Madeleine P. van Deventer and Elisabeth Knottenbelt (eds.), *Elisabeth Vreede. Ein Lebensbild*, p. 102.

51 Protokoll, p. 48. Goetheanum Archives.

52 Madeleine P. van Deventer, «Elisabeth Vreede. Zur 33. Wiederkehr ihres Todestages am 31. August». In *Nachrichtenblatt der Wochenschrift «Das Goetheanum»*, Aug. 22, p. 137.

53 Rudolf Steiner, *Die Weihnachtstagung zur Begründung der Allgemeinen Anthroposophischen Gesellschaft 1923/24*. CW 260, p. 57 [in English: *The Christmas Conference: For the Foundation of the General Anthroposophical Society, 1923/1924* (Anthroposophic Press, 1990].

54 In Madeleine P. van Deventer and Elisabeth Knottenbelt (eds.), *Elisabeth Vreede. Ein Lebensbild*, p. 15.

55 Ibid., p. 18.

56 Elisabeth Vreede, «Zur Geschichte des Rudolf Steiner Archivs am Goetheanum». Transcript of lecture. Stuttgart, Apr. 28, 1935. Unpublished. Goetheanum Archives, p. 4.

57 Rudolf Steiner, *Die Weihnachtstagung zur Begründung der Allgemeinen Anthroposophischen Gesellschaft 1923/24*. CW 260, p. 46 [in English: *The Christmas Conference: For the Foundation of the General Anthroposophical Society, 1923/1924* (Anthroposophic Press, 1990)].

58 Ibid., p. 94.

59 Rudolf Steiner, *Das Rätsel des Menschen. Die geistigen Hintergründe der menschlichen Geschichte.* CW 170. Dornach 1992, p. 260 [in English: *The Riddle of Humanity* (Mercury, 1990)].

60 Rudolf Steiner, *Die Weihnachtstagung zur Begründung der Allgemeinen Anthroposophischen Gesellschaft 1923/24.* CW 260, p. 271 [in English: *The Christmas Conference: For the Foundation of the General Anthroposophical Society, 1923/1924* (Anthroposophic Press, 1990)].

61 Rudolf Steiner, *Die Konstitution der Allgemeinen Anthroposophischen Gesellschaft und der Freien Hochschule für Geisteswissenschaft. Der Wiederaufbau des Goetheanum.* CW 260a, p. 380.

62 Cited in Peter Selg, *Elisabeth Vreede. 1879–1943.* Arlesheim 2009, p. 246 [in English: *Elisabeth Vreede: Adversity, Resilience, and Spiritual Science* (SteinerBooks, 2017)].

63 Elisabeth Vreede, «Zur Geschichte des Rudolf Steiner Archivs am Goetheanum», p. 6.

64 Elisabeth Vreede, *Zur Geschichte der Anthroposophischen Gesellschaft seit der Weihnachtstagung 1923.* Arlesheim 1935, p. 4.

65 Goetheanum Archives.

66 Letter to Karl Ballmer of March 30, 1935. Goetheanum Archives.

67 Letter to Maria Stiefelhagen of Aug. 8, 1935. Goetheanum Archives.

68 Cited in Lili Kolisko, *Eugen Kolisko. Ein Lebensbild. Zugleich ein Stück Geschichte der Anthroposophischen Gesellschaft.* Gerabronn-Crailsheim 1961, p. 306f.

69 Goetheanum Archives.

70 Letter to Miss Schünemann of Jan. 31, 1934. In Madeleine P. van Deventer and Elisabeth Knottenbelt (eds.), *Elisabeth Vreede. Ein Lebensbild*, p. 10.

71 Elisabeth Vreede, «Meine Vorstandsberufung» (my appointment to the Executive Council), typescript, Dec. 25, 1934. Unpublished. Goetheanum Archives, p. 5f.

72 Ita Wegman, Notebook entry, 1933 (Draft for her lecture in commemoration of Rudolf Steiner in London on Feb. 27, 1933), Ita Wegman Archives, Arlesheim. Cf. Emanuel Zeylmans van Emmichoven, *Wer war Ita Wegman. Eine Dokumentation,* vol. 1. Heidelberg 1990, p. 294ff [in English: *Who Was Ita Wegman: A Documentation,* vol. 1 (Mercury, 1995)]; and Peter Selg, *«Ich bleibe bei Ihnen». Rudolf Steiner und Ita Wegman. München, Pfingsten 1907. Dornach 1923–1925.* Stuttgart 2007, p. 44ff.

73 Facsimile, transcript, and context of this verse in Emanuel Zeylmans van Emmichoven, *Die Erkraftung des Herzens. Eine*

Mysterienschulung der Gegenwart. Rudolf Steiners Zusammenarbeit mit Ita Wegman. Arlesheim 2015, p. 404f.

74 Cited in Emanuel Zeylmans van Emmichoven, *Willem Zeylmans van Emmichoven. Ein Pionier der Anthroposophie.* Arlesheim 1979, p. 115f.

75 Rudolf Steiner, *Das Schicksalsjahr 1923 in der Geschichte der Anthroposophischen Gesellschaft. Vom Goetheanumbrand zur Weihnachtstagung.* CW 259. Dornach 1991, p. 484.

76 Ibid., p. 607.

77 Ita Wegman Archives, Arlesheim.

78 Letter to Maria Röschl of Feb. 22, 1935. Ita Wegman Archives, Arlesheim. The full letter was first published in Peter Selg, *Geistiger Widerstand und Überwindung. Ita Wegman 1933–1935.* Arlesheim 2005, p. 199ff [in English: *Spiritual Resistance: Ita Wegman, 1933–1935* (SteinerBooks, 2015)]. Many of the following citations from letters can be found in this monograph. On this see also Emanuel Zeylmans van Emmichoven's fundamental publication: *Wer war Ita Wegman. Eine Dokumentation, vol. 3. Kämpfe und Konflikte. 1924–1935.* Heidelberg 1992 [in English: *Who was Ita Wegman: A Documentation: Struggles and Conflicts, 1924 until 1935,* vol. 3 (Mercury, 2005)]

79 Ita Wegman Archives, Arlesheim.

80 Ibid.

81 Ita Wegman's letter to Nora Stein of Jan. 17, 1930. Ibid.

82 Ita Wegman's letter to Josef van Leer of Dec. 23, 1933. Ibid.

83 To Bernard Lievegoed, Feb. 14, 1935. Ibid.

84 Aug. 7, 1931. Ibid.

85 To Victor Thylmann, April 24, 1931. Ibid.

86 To Erich Liehr, Sept. 16, 1926. Ibid.

87 Letter to Maria Röschl of Feb. 22, 1935. Ibid.

88 Ita Wegman's notebook, No. 44 (draft letter), June 1934. Ibid.

89 Ibid.

90 June 10, 1937. Ibid.

91 Ibid.

92 Letter to Maria Röschl of Feb. 22, 1935. Ibid.

93 Ibid.

94 To George Adams Kaufmann, June 19, 1935. Ibid.

95 Cf. Peter Selg, *Die Freie Hochschule für Geisteswissenschaft und die Michael-Schule.* Arlesheim 2014, p. 67ff.

96 To Alice Wengraf, Jan. 31, 1935. Ita Wegman Archives, Arlesheim.

97 Ibid.

98 Ibid.

99 Liane Collot d'Herbois, «‹Jeder, der strebt, ist mein Freund.› Persönliche Erinnerungen an Ita Wegman.» In *Mitteilungen aus der anthroposophischen Arbeit in Deutschland,* issue 173, Michaelmas 1990, p. 113.

100 Ibid.

101 Cited in Emanuel Zeylmans van Emmichoven, *Wer war Ita Wegman. Eine Dokumentation,* vol. 2. Heidelberg 1990, p. 233 [in English: *Who was Ita Wegman: A Documentation, 1925 until 1943,* vol. 2 (Mercury, 2005)].

102 To Franz Löffler, Jan. 16, 1935. Ita Wegman Archives, Arlesheim.

103 Ibid.

104 To Mrs Weigmann, Jan. 7, 1931. Ita Wegman Archives, Arlesheim.

105 To Mathilde Enschedé, April 10, 1935. Ibid.

106 Guenther Wachsmuth, *Rudolf Steiners Erdenleben und Wirken. Von der Jahrhundertwende bis zum Tode. Die Geburt der Geisteswissenschaft. Eine Biographie.* Dornach 1951, p. 567 [in English: *The Life and Work of Rudolf Steiner: From the Turn of the Century to His Death* (Garber, 1989)].

107 Rudolf Steiner, *Soziales Verständnis aus geisteswissenschaftlicher Erkenntnis. Die geistigen Hintergründe der sozialen Frage,* vol 3. CW 191. Dornach 1989, p. 122.

108 Guenther Wachsmuth, *Rudolf Steiners Erdenleben und Wirken. Von der Jahrhundertwende bis zum Tode*, p. 412 [in English: *The Life and Work of Rudolf Steiner: From the Turn of the Century to His Death* (Garber, 1989)].

109 Rudolf Steiner, *Mantrische Sprüche. Seelenübungen*, vol. 2. CW 268, p. 257 [in English: *Soul Exercises: Word and Symbol Meditations, 1903–1924* (SteinerBooks, 2015)].

110 In Heinz Herbert Schöffler, *Guenther Wachsmuth. Ein Lebensbild.* Dornach 1995, p. 225.

111 In *Mitteilungen aus dem anthroposophischen Leben in der Schweiz,* special issue 6. Christmas 2000, p. 24.

112 Guenther Wachsmuth, *Rudolf Steiners Erdenleben und Wirken. Von der Jahrhundertwende bis zum Tode*, p. 415.

113 In *Mitteilungen aus dem anthroposophischen Leben in der Schweiz,* special issue 6, p. 24.

114 In Heinz Herbert Schöffler, *Guenther Wachsmuth. Ein Lebensbild,* p. 203.

115 Guenther Wachsmuth, *Rudolf Steiners Erdenleben und Wirken. Von der Jahrhundertwende bis zum Tode*, p. 623 [in English: *The Life and Work of Rudolf Steiner: From the Turn of the Century to His Death* (Garber, 1989)].

116 Guenther Wachsmuth, «Das neue Goetheanum». Lecture to members. Hamburg, May 1926. In *Mitteilungen aus dem anthroposophischen Leben in der Schweiz,* special issue 6, p. 119.

117 Heinz Herbert Schöffler, *Guenther Wachsmuth. Ein Lebensbild*, p. 227.

118 Albert Steffen, diary entry of April 25, 1956. Ibid., p. 194.

119 In *Mitteilungen aus dem anthroposophischen Leben in der Schweiz,* special issue 6, p. 65.

120 Ibid., p. 41.

121 Ibid., p. 123.

122 Rudolf Steiner / Marie Steiner-von Sivers, *Briefwechsel und Dokumente. 1901–1925.* CW 262, p. 452 [in English: *Correspondence and Documents 1901–1925* (Anthroposophic Press, 1988)].

123 Guenther Wachsmuth, *Rudolf Steiners Erdenleben und Wirken. Von der Jahrhundertwende bis zum Tode*, p. 624 [in English: *The Life and Work of Rudolf Steiner: From the Turn of the Century to His Death* (Garber, 1989)].

124 Heinz Herbert Schöffler, *Guenther Wachsmuth. Ein Lebensbild,* p. 125.

125 Guenther Wachsmuth, «Das neue Goetheanum». Lecture to members. Hamburg, May 1926. In *Mitteilungen aus dem anthroposophischen Leben in der Schweiz,* special issue 6, p. 131.

126 Guenther Wachsmuth, Schatzmeisterbericht 1939. Cited in Heinz Herbert Schöffler, *Guenther Wachsmuth. Ein Lebensbild,* p. 133.

127 Ibid., p. 217.

128 Facsimile and transcript of this letter. Ibid., p. 232-233.

129 Ibid., p. 225.

130 Ibid., p. 226.

131 Rudolf Steiner, *Die Polarität von Dauer und Entwicklung im Menschenleben.* CW 184. Dornach 2002, p. 295.

132 Albert Steffen, Diary entry of March 4, 1963. In Heinz Herbert Schöffler, *Guenther Wachsmuth. Ein Lebensbild,* p. 216.

133 Albert Steffen, Diary entry of Oct. 4, 1957. Ibid., p. 197.

134 Johann Peter Eckermann, *Gespräche mit Goethe in den letzten Jahren seines Lebens.* Leipzig 1885, p. 265.

135 In Heinz Herbert Schöffler, *Guenther Wachsmuth. Ein Lebensbild,* p. 229.

136 Albert Steffen, Diary entry of March 2, 1963. Ibid., p. 216.

137 Rudolf Steiner, *Unsere Toten. Ansprachen, Gedenkworte und Meditationssprüche. 1906–1924.* CW 261. Dornach 1984, p. 293 [in English: *Our Dead: Memorial, Funeral, and Cremation Addresses* (SteinerBooks, 2011)].

138 Rudolf Steiner, *Four Mystery Dramas, The Portal of Initiation.* SteinerBooks, 2015, tr. R. and H. Pusch, p. 145.
139 Diary entry of April 10, 1910, Albert Steffen Foundation. In Peter Selg, *Albert Steffen. Begegnung mit Rudolf Steiner.* Dornach 2009, p. 49.
140 Cited in Heinz Matile, «‹Ich forschte nicht nach dem, was ein Mensch lehrte, sondern nach dem, was er lebte.› Zu Albert Steffens Verhältnis und Beitrag zur Anthroposophie». In *Hinweise und Studien zum Lebenswerk von Albert Steffen*, issue 12/13, Michaelmas 1992, p. 7.
141 Albert Steffen, *Begegnungen mit Rudolf Steiner.* Dornach 1975, p. 101.
142 Albert Steffen, *Auf Geisteswegen.* Dornach 1942, p. 53f.
143 Diary entry of July 19, 1920. Cited in Heinz Matile, «‹Ich forschte nicht nach dem, was ein Mensch lehrte, sondern nach dem, was er lebte.› Zu Albert Steffens Verhältnis und Beitrag zur Anthroposophie». In *Hinweise und Studien zum Lebenswerk von Albert Steffen*, issue 12/13, p. 10.
144 Albert Steffen, *Begegnungen mit Rudolf Steiner.* Dornach 1975, p. 192.
145 Ibid., p. 193.
146 Albert Steffen, *Geistige Heimat.* Dornach 1941, p. 6.
147 Albert Steffen, *Begegnungen mit Rudolf Steiner.* Dornach 1975, p. 207.
148 Rudolf Steiner, *Die Weihnachtstagung zur Begründung der Allgemeinen Anthroposophischen Gesellschaft 1923/24.* CW 260, p. 31 [in English: *The Christmas Conference: For the Foundation of the General Anthroposophical Society, 1923/1924* (Anthroposophic Press, 1990)].
149 Albert Steffen, «Ansprache zum siebenten Todestage Rudolf Steiners» (March 30, 1932). In *Geistesschulung und Gemeinschaftsbildung.* Dornach 1974, p. 297.
150 Albert Steffen, *Geistesschulung und Gemeinschaftsbildung*, p. 146.
151 Albert Steffen, «Erinnerung» (Mai 1934). In *Geistesschulung und Gemeinschaftsbildung*, p. 319.
152 Sept. 3, 1939. Ibid., p. 404f.
153 Albert Steffen, *Aus dem Fragment «Stiftungsdrama».* Dornach 2016, p. 56.
154 Albert Steffen, «Ansprache am 3, Sept. 1939 anlässlich der katastrophalen Zeitereignisse». In *Geistesschulung und Gemeinschaftsbildung*, p. 404f.

155 Rudolf Steiner, *Die Konstitution der Allgemeinen Anthroposophischen Gesellschaft und der Freien Hochschule für Geisteswissenschaft. Der Wiederaufbau des Goetheanum.* CW 260a, p. 33f. Cf: Rudolf Steiner, *Architecture as Peacework: The First Goetheanum, Dornach, 1914* (SteinerBooks, 2016).

156 Albert Steffen, «Ansprache am 3. Sept. 1939 anlässlich der katastrophalen Zeitereignisse». In *Geistesschulung und Gemeinschaftsbildung,* p. 413.

157 Rudolf Steiner, *Die Konstitution der Allgemeinen Anthroposophischen Gesellschaft und der Freien Hochschule für Geisteswissenschaft. Der Wiederaufbau des Goetheanum.* CW 260a, p. 78.

158 Albert Steffen, «Ansprache zum siebenten Todestage Rudolf Steiners» (March 30, 1932). In *Geistesschulung und Gemeinschaftsbildung.* Dornach 1974, p. 298.

159 Rudolf Steiner, *Die Geschichte und die Bedingungen der anthroposophischen Bewegung im Verhältnis zur Anthroposophischen Gesellschaft.* CW 258. Dornach 1981, p. 141 [in English: *The Anthroposophic Movement* (Rudolf Steiner Press, 1993)].

160 Albert Steffen, «Ansprache zum siebenten Todestage Rudolf Steiners» (March 30, 1932). In *Geistesschulung und Gemeinschaftsbildung,* p. 300.

161 Albert Steffen, *Aus dem Fragment «Stiftungsdrama»,* p. 34.

162 «Das Stiftungsdrama im Tagebuch». Ibid., p. 17.

163 Albert Steffen, «Aus dem Merkbuch eines Erkenntnissuchers». In *Geistesschulung und Gemeinschaftsbildung,* p. 532.

164 Albert Steffen, «Geistgemeinschaft». Ibid., p. 676f.

165 Albert Steffen, *In memoriam Rudolf Steiner.* Basel 1927, p. 5f., tr. Matthew Barton.

166 Rudolf Steiner, *Esoterische Betrachtungen karmischer Zusammenhänge*, vol. 6. CW 240. Dornach 1992, p. 179.

167 Ibid., p. 145.

168 Rudolf Steiner, *Die Bhagavad Gita und die Paulusbriefe.* CW 142. Dornach 1982, p. 125 [in English: *The Bhagavad Gita and the West: The Esoteric Significance of the Bhagavad Gita and Its Relation to the Epistles of Paul* (SteinerBooks, 2006)].

169 Rudolf Steiner, *Anthroposophie, ihre Erkenntniswurzeln und Lebensfrüchte.* CW 78. Dornach 1986, p. 150.

170 "If you look into the world today, there is—and has been for years—an enormous amount of destructive potential. There are forces at work that give us a glimpse of the abysses Western civilization is heading toward." (*Die Weihnachtstagung zur Begründung der Allgemeinen Anthroposophischen Gesellschaft 1923/24.*

CW 260, p. 270 [in English: *The Christmas Conference: For the Foundation of the General Anthroposophical Society, 1923/1924* (Anthroposophic Press, 1990)].)

171 Rudolf Steiner, *Anthroposophische Gemeinschaftsbildung*. CW 257. Dornach 1989, p. 154 [in English: *Awakening to Community* (SteinerBooks, 1975)].

172 Ibid., p. 84.

173 Rudolf Steiner, *Mantrische Sprüche. Seelenübungen*, vol. 2. CW 268. Dornach 1999, p. 346 [in English: *Soul Exercises: Word and Symbol Meditations, 1903–1924* (SteinerBooks, 2015)].

174 Rudolf Steiner, *Wege zu einem neuen Baustil. «Und der Bau wird Mensch»*. CW 286. Dornach 1982, p. 62 [in English: *Architecture as a Synthesis of the Arts* (Rudolf Steiner Press, 1999)].

175 Rudolf Steiner, *Four Mystery Dramas*. CW 14. *The Guardian of the Threshold*, p. 120. Tr. R. and H. Pusch.

176 In *Hinweise und Studien zum Lebenswerk von Albert Steffen*, issue 18/19, p. 35.

177 *Aus dem Fragment «Stiftungsdrama»*, p. 34.

178 Oct. 16, 1931. Albert Steffen-Stiftung, Dornach.

179 Albert Steffen, *Am Kreuzweg des Schicksals*. Dornach 1952, p. 89, tr. Matthew Barton.

2. The Anthroposophical Society and Its Relationship to the Spiritual World

1 Jan Patočka, «Plato und Europa». In *Ausgewählte Schriften*. Stuttgart 1987—1992.

2 Cf. Ita Wegman, Notes for an address, circa 1927. In Emanuel Zeylmans van Emmichoven, *Wer war Ita Wegman. Eine Dokumentation*, vol. 1, p. 122. On the situation in the Anthroposophical Society in 1922, before the Goetheanum fire, cf. Peter Selg, *Die Identität der Allgemeinen Anthroposophischen Gesellschaft*. Arlesheim 2012, p. 15ff. and Peter Selg, *Rudolf Steiner. 1861–1925. Lebens- und Werkgeschichte*, vol. 3. Arlesheim 2012, pp. 1655ff.

3 Rudolf Steiner, *Menschenwesen, Menschenschicksal und Welt-Entwicklung*. CW 226. Dornach 1988, p. 134.

4 Rudolf Steiner, *Die Weihnachtstagung zur Begründung der Allgemeinen Anthroposophischen Gesellschaft 1923/24*. CW 260, p. 284 [in English: *The Christmas Conference: For the Foundation of the General Anthroposophical Society, 1923/1924* (Anthroposophic Press, 1990)].

5 Rudolf Steiner, *Die soziale Grundforderung unserer Zeit—In geänderter Zeitlage (1918)*. CW 186. Dornach 1990, p. 122.

6 Matthew 18:20

7 Rudolf Steiner / Marie Steiner-von Sivers, *Briefwechsel und Dokumente. 1901–1925*. CW 262. Dornach 2002, p. 125 [in English: *Correspondence and Documents, 1901–1925* (Anthroposophic Press, 1988)].

8 Rudolf Steiner, *Anthroposophische Gemeinschaftsbildung*. CW 257. Dornach 1989, p. 31 [in English: *Awakening to Community* (Anthroposophic Press, 1975)].

9 Rudolf Steiner, *Die Weihnachtstagung zur Begründung der Allgemeinen Anthroposophischen Gesellschaft 1923/24*. CW 260, p. 35 [in English: *The Christmas Conference: For the Foundation of the General Anthroposophical Society, 1923/1924* (Anthroposophic Press, 1990)].

10 Rudolf Steiner, *Anthroposophische Gemeinschaftsbildung*. CW 257. Dornach 1989, p. 112 [in English: *Awakening to Community* (Anthroposophic Press, 1975)].

11 Ibid., p. 114.

12 Ibid., p. 117.

13 Rudolf Steiner, *Vorträge und Kurse über christlich-religiöses Wirken, V. Apokalypse und Priesterwirken*. CW 346. Dornach 2001, p. 21 [in English: *The Book of Revelation: And the Work of the Priest* (Rudolf Steiner Press, 1999)].

14 Rudolf Steiner, *Makrokosmos und Mikrokosmos. Die große und die kleine Welt. Seelenfragen, Lebensfragen, Geistesfragen*. CW 119. Dornach 1988, p. 122 [in English: *Macrocosm and Microcosm* (Rudolf Steiner Press, 1968)].

15 Ibid.

16 Rudolf Steiner, *Die Weihnachtstagung zur Begründung der Allgemeinen Anthroposophischen Gesellschaft 1923/24*. CW 260, p. 115 [in English: *The Christmas Conference: For the Foundation of the General Anthroposophical Society, 1923/1924* (Anthroposophic Press, 1990)].

17 Rudolf Steiner, *Das Geheimnis des Todes. Wesen und Bedeutung Mitteleuropas und die europäischen Volksgeister*. CW 159. Dornach 2005, p. 328.

18 Ibid.

19 Ibid., p. 321.

20 Rudolf Steiner, *Das Hereinwirken geistiger Wesenheiten in den Menschen (1908)*. CW 102. Dornach 2001, p. 195.

21 Rudolf Steiner, Anthroposophische Gemeinschaftsbildung. CW 257. Dornach 1989, p. 25 [in English: *Awakening to Community* (Anthroposophic Press, 1975)].

22 Ibid., p. 13.

3. My Existential Relationship with the Anthroposophical Society

1 Dornach, Sept. 23, 1924. Cf. Rudolf Steiner, *Esoterische Betrachtungen karmischer Zusammenhänge,* vol. 4. CW 238. Dornach 1991.

4. The Universal Temple

1 Rudolf Steiner, *Four Mystery Dramas,* p. 235.

2 Johann Wolfgang von Goethe, *Das Märchen von der grünen Schlange und der schönen Lilie.* Dornach 1982, p. 39. English translation by Thomas Carlyle.

3 Cf. Johannes Greiner, *Es ist alles ganz anders.* Hamburg 2015.

4 In Rudolf Steiner, *Die Weihnachtstagung zur Begründung der Allgemeinen Anthroposophischen Gesellschaft 1923/1924.* CW 260, p. 18 [in English: *The Christmas Conference: For the Foundation of the General Anthroposophical Society, 1923/1924* (Anthroposophic Press, 1990)].

5 Heinz Eckhoff, *Schicksal der Menschheit an der Schwelle. Anthroposophie in den Entscheidungen unserer Zeit.* Stuttgart 1998, p. 94.

6 Mario Betti wrote, very aptly, “Loyalty to a person, which is entirely understandable and noble in itself, can only cause division in a society of many. Loyalty to the factual ideal of a Christ-inspired community that remains effective when contrasting views meet and always encourages dialog I consider to be of higher value.” (*Leben im Geiste der Anthroposophie. Eine Autobiografie.* Arlesheim 2015, p. 198.)

7 Rudolf Steiner, *Der innere Aspekt des sozialen Rätsels.* CW 193. Dornach 2007, p. 48.

8 Albert Steffen, *Der Sturz des Antichrist.* Dornach 1993, p. 9.

9 Rudolf Steiner, *Four Mystery Dramas, The Trial of the Soul*, p. 226, tr. R. and H. Pusch.

10 Ibid. p. 106.

11 In the first scene of the first drama, *The Portal of Initiation.*

12 *Four Mystery Dramas, The Trial of the Soul*, p. 236.

13 Ibid. pp. 234–235.

14 Mario Betti, *Leben im Geiste der Anthroposophie. Eine Autobiografie.* Arlesheim 2015, p. 243.

15 *The Trial of the Soul*, pp. 244–245.

16 This chapter is from a revised introduction to the evening performance on Feb. 13, 2016, with scenes from the mystery dramas. Gioia Falk chose passages from *The Trial of the Soul,* the second mystery drama (scenes 6 to 9); and from *The Souls' Awakening,* the fourth drama (scene 6) to create a program entitled "The Common Temple." Her intention was to deepen and enrich the conference theme by offering viewers the possibility to experience these scenes in artistic performances.

5. "Cosmic Midnight Hour"

1 Rudolf Steiner, *Four Mystery Dramas*, p. 489.

2 Ibid., pp. 490–492.

3 Ibid., pp. 233–234.

4 Ibid., p. 235.

5 Ibid., p. 256.

6 Ibid., p. 75f.

7 Ibid., pp. 478–479.

6. The Evolving Body of the Anthroposophical Society

1 Rudolf Steiner, *Wie erlangt man Erkenntnisse der höheren Welten?* CW 10. Dornach 2010, p. 161.

2 Rudolf Steiner, *Die Weihnachtstagung zur Begründung der Allgemeinen Anthroposophischen Gesellschaft 1923/24*. CW 260, p. 270 [in English: *The Christmas Conference: For the Foundation of the General Anthroposophical Society, 1923/1924* (Anthroposophic Press, 1990)].

3 Rudolf Steiner, *Vergangenheits- und Zukunftsimpulse im sozialen Geschehen*. CW 190. Dornach 1980, p. 146f.

4 Rudolf Steiner, *Mysterienstätten des Mittelalters*. CW 233a. Dornach 1991, p. 82.

5 Rudolf Steiner, *Die spirituellen Hintergründe der äußeren Welt. Der Sturz der Geister der Finsternis*. CW 177. Dornach, 1999, p. 170ff. [in English: *The Fall of the Spirits of Darkness* (Rudolf Steiner Press, 1993)].

6 From Section 1 of the original bylaws of the Anthroposophical Society. In Rudolf Steiner, *Die Weihnachtstagung zur Begründung der Allgemeinen Anthroposophischen Gesellschaft 1923/24*. CW 260, p. 48 [in English: *The Christmas Conference: For the*

Foundation of the General Anthroposophical Society, 1923/1924 (Anthroposophic Press, 1990)].

7 Ibid., p. 280.

8 Rudolf Steiner, *Esoterische Betrachtungen karmischer Zusammenhänge*, vol. 3. CW 237. Dornach 1991, p. 142.

9 Ibid., p. 151.

10 Ibid., p. 173.

11 Rudolf Steiner, *Das Johannes-Evangelium*. CW 103. Dornach 1995, p. 151 [in English: *The Gospel of St. John* (Anthroposophic Press, 1940)].

12 Ibid., p. 168.

13 Rudolf Steiner, *Die Welträtsel und die Anthroposophie*. CW 54. Dornach 1983, p. 193.

14 Rudolf Steiner, *Betriebsräte und Sozialisierung*. CW 331. Dornach 1989, p. 79.

15 There is, to my knowledge, to this day no recognized juristic personhood that requires this balance between an initiative and its acceptance. In principle it is the general meeting that has the final say and power, and that appoints those who bear responsibility for the initiative. The archetype of the Anthroposophical Society can be realized in various forms, however. We could aim to introduce the form created by the Christmas Conference into the legal sphere; it would then in future no longer be the shareholders who decide on the future of a joint stock company, nor would the members decide about the future of a society. Such decisions would be taken jointly by those who bear the responsibility and those who support them.

16 Rudolf Steiner, *Die Weihnachtstagung zur Begründung der Allgemeinen Anthroposophischen Gesellschaft 1923/24*. CW 260, p. 280 [in English: *The Christmas Conference: For the Foundation of the General Anthroposophical Society, 1923/1924* (Anthroposophic Press, 1990)].

17 Ibid., p. 281.

18 Cf. Marc Desaules, «Öffentlich-esoterisch: die Dynamik der neuen Sozialgestalt». In Peter Selg and Marc Desaules (eds.), *Die Sozialgestalt der Weihnachtstagung*. Arlesheim 2014, p. 41ff.

19 Rudolf Steiner, *Wahrspruchworte*. CW 40. Dornach 2005, p. 109 [in English: *Truth-Wrought-Words* (Anthroposophic Press 1979)].

Books in English Translation by Peter Selg

On Rudolf Steiner

Rudolf Steiner: Life and Work *(1923): The Burning of the Goetheanum,* vol. 6 of 7 (2018)

Rudolf Steiner: Life and Work *(1919–1922): Social Threefolding and the Waldorf School,* vol. 5 of 7 (2017)

Rudolf Steiner: Life and Work *(1914–1918): The Years of World War I,* vol. 4 of 7 (2016)

Rudolf Steiner: Life and Work *(1900–1914): Spiritual Science and Spiritual Community,* vol. 3 of 7 (2015)

Rudolf Steiner: Life and Work *(1890–1900): Weimar and Berlin,* vol. 2 of 7 (2014)

Rudolf Steiner: Life and Work *(1861–1890): Childhood, Youth, and Study Years,* vol. 1 of 7 (2014)

Rudolf Steiner and Christian Rosenkreutz (2012)

Rudolf Steiner as a Spiritual Teacher: *From Recollections of Those Who Knew Him* (2010)

On Christology

Rudolf Steiner and The Christian Community (2018)

The Sufferings of the Nathan Soul: *Anthroposophic Christology on the Eve of World War I* (2016)

The Lord's Prayer and Rudolf Steiner: *A Study of His Insights into the Archetypal Prayer of Christianity* (2014)

The Creative Power of Anthroposophical Christology: *An Outline of Occult Science · The First Goetheanum · The Fifth Gospel · The Christmas Conference* (with Sergei O. Prokofieff) (2012)

Christ and the Disciples: *The Destiny of an Inner Community* (2012)

The Figure of Christ: *Rudolf Steiner and the Spiritual Intention behind the Goetheanum's Central Work of Art* (2009)

Rudolf Steiner and the Fifth Gospel: *Insights into a New Understanding of the Christ Mystery* (2010)

Seeing Christ in Sickness and Healing (2005)

On General Anthroposophy

The Anthroposophical Society: *The Understanding and Continued Activity of the Christmas Conference* (edited with Marc Desaules) (2018)

Elisabeth Vreede: *Adversity, Resilience, and Spiritual Science* (2017)

The Michael School: *And the School of Spiritual Science* (2016)

The Destiny of the Michael Community: *Foundation Stone for the Future* (2014)

Spiritual Resistance: *Ita Wegman 1933–1935* (2014)

The Last Three Years: *Ita Wegman in Ascona, 1940–1943* (2014)

From Gurs to Auschwitz: *The Inner Journey of Maria Krehbiel-Darmstädter* (2013)

Crisis in the Anthroposophical Society: *And Pathways to the Future* (with Sergei O. Prokofieff) (2013)

Rudolf Steiner's Foundation Stone Meditation: *And the Destruction of the Twentieth Century* (2013)

The Culture of Selflessness: *Rudolf Steiner, the Fifth Gospel, and the Time of Extremes* (2012)

The Mystery of the Heart: *The Sacramental Physiology of the Heart in Aristotle, Thomas Aquinas, and Rudolf Steiner* (2012)

Rudolf Steiner and the School for Spiritual Science: *The Foundation of the "First Class"* (2012)

Rudolf Steiner's Intentions for the Anthroposophical Society: *The Executive Council, the School for Spiritual Science, and the Sections* (2011)

The Fundamental Social Law: *Rudolf Steiner on the Work of the Individual and the Spirit of Community* (2011)

The Path of the Soul after Death: *The Community of the Living and the Dead as Witnessed by Rudolf Steiner in His Eulogies and Farewell Addresses* (2011)

The Agriculture Course, Koberwitz, Whitsun 1924: *Rudolf Steiner and the Beginnings of Biodynamics* (2010)

On Anthroposophical Medicine and Curative Education

The Warmth Meditation: *A Path to the Good in the Service of Healing* (2016)

Honoring Life: *Medical Ethics and Physician-Assisted Suicide* (2014); with Sergei O. Prokofieff

I Am for Going Ahead: *Ita Wegman's Work for the Social Ideals of Anthroposophy* (2012)

The Child with Special Needs: *Letters and Essays on Curative Education* (ed.) (2009)

Ita Wegman and Karl König: *Letters and Documents* (2008)

Karl König's Path to Anthroposophy (2008)

Karl König: My Task: *Autobiography and Biographies* (Ed.) (2008)

On Child Development and Waldorf Education

The Child as a Sense Organ: *An Anthroposophic Understanding of the Imitation Processes* (2017)

I Am Different from You: *How Children Experience Themselves and the World in the Middle of Childhood* (2011)

Unbornness: *Human Pre-existence and the Journey toward Birth* (2010)

The Essence of Waldorf Education (2010)

The Therapeutic Eye: *How Rudolf Steiner Observed Children* (2008)

A Grand Metamorphosis: *Contributions to the Spiritual-Scientific Anthropology and Education of Adolescents* (2008)

Ita Wegman Institute
for Basic Research into Anthroposophy

Pfeffinger Weg 1a, ch 4144 Arlesheim, Switzerland
www.wegmaninstitut.ch
e-mail: sekretariat@wegmaninstitut.ch

The Ita Wegman Institute for Basic Research into Anthroposophy is a non-profit research and teaching organization. It undertakes basic research into the lifework of Dr. Rudolf Steiner (1861–1925) and the application of Anthroposophy in specific areas of life, especially medicine, education, and curative education. Work carried out by the Institute is supported by a number of foundations and organizations and an international group of friends and supporters. The Director of the Institute is Prof. Dr. Peter Selg.

A Note from SteinerBooks

SteinerBooks is a 501(c)(3) not-for-profit organization, incorporated in New York State since 1928 to promote the progress and welfare of humanity and to increase public awareness of Rudolf Steiner (1861–1925), the Austrian-born polymath writer, lecturer, spiritual scientist, philosopher, cosmologist, educator, psychologist, alchemist, ecologist, Christian mystic, comparative religionist, and evolutionary theorist, who was the creator of Anthroposophy ("human wisdom") as a path uniting the spiritual in the human being with the spiritual in the universe; and to this end publish and distribute books for adults and children, utilize the electronic media, hold conferences, and engage in similar activities making available his works and exploring themes arising from, and related to, them and the movement that he founded.

- We commission translations of books by Rudolf Steiner unpublished in English, as well as new translations for updated editions.
- Our aim is to make works on Anthroposophy available to all by publishing and distributing both introductory and advanced works on spiritual research.
- New books are published for both print and digital editions to reach the widest possible readership.
- Recent technology also makes it efficient for us to make our previously out-of-print works available for the next generation.

SteinerBooks depends on our readers' financial support, which is greatly needed, appreciated, and tax-deductible. Please consider a donation by check or other means to SteinerBooks, 610 Main St., Great Barrington, MA 01230. We accept donations via PayPal at www.steinerbooks.org. For more information about supporting our work, send email to friends@steinerbooks.org or call 413-528-8233.